Territorial Development and Action Research

This book is part of the Project Gipuzkoa Sarean, fostered by the Provincial Council of Gipuzkoa and developed under Orkestra's academic supervision.

Gipuzkoako Foru Aldundia

BASQUE INSTITUTE
OF COMPETITIVENESS
DEUSTO FOUNDATION

UNIVERSITY OF AGDER

Territorial Development and Action Research

Innovation Through Dialogue

JAMES KARLSEN
University of Agder, Norway

MIREN LARREA
Orkestra-Basque Institute of Competitiveness, Spain

Routledge
Taylor & Francis Group

LONDON AND NEW YORK

First published 2014 by Gower Publishing

Published 2016 by Routledge
2 Park Square, Milton Park, Abingdon, Oxfordshire OX14 4RN
711 Third Avenue, New York, NY 10017, USA

First issued in paperback 2016

Routledge is an imprint of the Taylor & Francis Group, an informa business

Gower Applied Business Research
Our programme provides leaders, practitioners, scholars and researchers with thought
provoking, cutting edge books that combine conceptual insights, interdisciplinary rigour and
practical relevance in key areas of business and management.

British Library Cataloguing in Publication Data
A catalogue record for this book is available from the British Library.

Library of Congress Cataloging-in-Publication Data
Karlsen, James.
    Territorial development and action research : innovation through dialogue / by James
Karlsen and Miren Larrea.
        pages cm
    Includes bibliographical references and index.
    ISBN 978-1-4724-0923-2 (hardback : alk. paper)
1. Regional planning. 2. Action research. I. Larrea, Miren.
II. Title.

    HT391.K35 2014
    307.1'2 – dc23

                                                                        2013040868

ISBN 13: 978-1-138-27198-2 (pbk)

ISBN 13: 978-1-4724-0923-2 (hbk)

We dedicate this book to Ellen and Mikel, the backstage crew in this performance. Without your efforts, we would not have been able to finish it. To Leandro and Kontxi, we agree with you that we should not write another one for a while. To Libe, Edurne and Malen, we promise that there will be more time for you now. To Enok, Andreas, Sindre and Jon-Henrik, thanks for your support throughout the writing process.

Contents

PART III INNOVATION THROUGH DIALOGUE

List of Figures

List of Tables

About the Authors

James Karlsen (PhD Norwegian University of Science and Technology) has worked with territorial development processes as a policy maker and a researcher at national and local level in Norway and the Basque Country, Spain. He is now an Associate Professor at University of Agder. When the book was written he was a senior researcher at Agderforskning and at Orkestra, the Basque Institute of Competitiveness. Karlsen is widely published on topics such as regional innovation systems, action research, networks, the role of universities in regional development, and how regions can construct regional advantage.

Miren Larrea (PhD University of Deusto) started her career as research assistant at the University of Deusto, where she focused her research on local production systems. After a decade dedicated to teaching and research, she left university to work as a practitioner in a local development agency. Later she returned to the university system at Orkestra, the Basque Institute of Competitiveness, where she is now senior researcher. She has published in international journals and books on networks for territorial development, local development agencies, governance, and action research as a strategy for connecting research and policy.

Preface

We cannot remember exactly when we decided to write this book. What we know for sure is that this version has little to do with the original idea that launched the project. It has been a long and hard process of self-reflection, and the outcome, if not a surprise, has been something we could have not imagined when we started.

The initial motivation was to provide some basic text for training processes on action research, to be used with researchers and practitioners. We soon saw that the world did not need a manual on action research from us. However, we had a feeling that we had learnt something that was valuable, and the process of trying to discover what we had learnt began. There were stages in the process when we thought this was a book about action research, and stages when we were sure it was a book about regional innovation systems. After this long process, we realise it is a book about action research in territorial development.

We have not seen any other book with this title or topic. We feel this is a field that needs to be explored, and we hope that our experiences and reflections are of relevance for those who are participating in territorial development processes and for those who are studying them. We know that we are not the only ones who have faced the types of challenges we are reflecting on in this book.

Our position on action research and territorial development is within the pragmatic tradition. Through our reflection from experience and by connecting this to theoretical discussions, we also want to demonstrate the possible useful and practical consequences of our discussion.

There are two authors behind this first-person plural *we*, so there are compound motivations and rationales for the book. One half of *we*, James Karlsen, had worked for twelve years as a policy maker before he entered the research path. After working in applied research for some years he joined a PhD programme in action research at the Norwegian University of Science and Technology. As a civil servant he had learnt that decision making processes are much more complex, complicated and messy than is usually believed in universities. As a PhD student he learned to question and reflect on practice. So when, in 2008, he made the decision to join a research group around two thousand kilometres away from home with the aim of contributing to creating an action research environment, he knew about the complexity of the challenge. He also knew about the impossibility of bringing recipes for success, which he suspected was expected of him.

The second half of *we*, Miren Larrea, started her professional career in the University of Deusto, where she focused on research on regional and local development for a decade. She then left her full-time position at the university to work in a local development agency on the creation of a co-operation network for territorial development. At that time some of her fellow researchers felt it was mistake, a step that would take her away from her research path. Eleven years later this decision is analysed in the book as one of the elements that fostered the creation of an action research environment in Orkestra, the Basque Institute for Competitiveness, where she is now a senior researcher. Making this experience valuable for academics who want to get engaged in action and practitioners who are interested in connecting to research is one of the challenges she faces with this book.

In writing this book we think that it is possible to learn from situations, from experience, which in the context of the book means that it is possible to learn from what we have lived through. Today, policy makers want to obtain more useful knowledge from research. Researchers participate more than ever in projects with practitioners involved in territorial development. But the practical knowing developed in these contexts barely transcends the agents participating in the process. This is our attempt to do so.

It has not been easy to write this book. We have had times when we have struggled and nearly given up on the project, and there have been other times when it has been fun to work on the book. We are different in many respects – gender, age, culture and education. The differences between us have been among the strengths that gave us the energy to write the book. The differences between us showed us that there were different approaches to understanding territorial development and that our taken-for-granted assumptions could be used as a strength in the writing process. The burning aim of writing from experience, of writing a different story on territorial development processes, has been a common foundation for both of us.

We have had support from many colleagues throughout the writing process – researchers as well as practitioners. We thank Mari Jose Aranguren for always believing in this book. We thank Morten Levin for his feedback on some of the chapters, but especially for encouraging us to continue writing when we approached him early on in this process; Bjørn Gustavsen and Øyvind Pålshaugen for taking time to discuss with us; Arne Isaksen, Hans Christian Garmann Johnsen and Markku Sotarauta for their feedback on various chapters, and the participants in the workshop in Kristiansand in June 2012, especially Bjørn T. Asheim, who reinforced our desire to write on regional innovation systems inside out.

We thank the territorial actors with whom we worked and learnt in the cases presented and also in the process of writing this book: Itziar Abarisketa, Jesus Agirre, Asier Aranbarri, Mari Jose Aranguren, Ainhoa Arrona, Ander Arzelus, Amaia Azpiazu, Xabier Barandiaran, Begoña Beobide, Miren Estensoro, Mikel Navarro, Haritz Salaberria, James R. Wilson and Jon Zubizarreta. It has been an amazing learning process.

We want to thank Patricia Canto and Lorea Yarzabal for their help with the typescript and drawing of figures, and Leanne Benneworth for help with the language.

We want to thank Orkestra, the Basque Institute of Competitiveness; Agderforskning, the Centre for Advanced Studies in Regional Innovation Strategies at the University of Agder, and the Provincial Council of Gipuzkoa for supporting us and funding the writing process of the book.

We also want to thank the editorial team from Gower for their good collaboration throughout the process.

Finally, we want to thank the people in our lives who have helped us see the beauty in words, communication and dialogue. Most of them are not visible in our professional careers as we shared parallel conversations in the outland of research. They helped us understand that, at the end of the day, most things have to do with human nature and our need to communicate.

Introduction

This book is written in the intersection of territorial development (TD) and action research (AR). Our main thesis is that territorial development is constructed through the engagement of the people living and working in the territory. Innovation, which we will relate closely to development, is a result of social processes. We believe that people have the ability to break historical trends and patterns and establish new institutions and economic order. Action research fits with this approach to territorial development because action research is research carried out in real time with participants in change processes. We also believe that researchers, research organisations and universities have a responsibility to engage in their host territories. It is through participation, collaboration and responsible engagement that a common future can be constructed. This can only be done through micro actions by people who trust each other and are aligned despite having conflicting perspectives. There are no recipes for territorial development. Territories are different, and it is not possible to copy and paste successful policies. One-size innovation policies do not fit all territories (Tödtling and Trippl, 2005), and learning from differences is as important as learning from success (Ennals and Gustavsen, 1999). One of the roles of research is to engage in territorial development processes with policy makers and other regional actors so that a socially responsible common future can be created for the people who are working and living in a territory.

Why This Book?

There is a wide range of literature by a large group of researchers studying innovation, competitiveness and territorial development, and there is an ongoing political discourse about these issues. The stream of concepts within this literature is rapid and overwhelming (Lagendijk, 2006). Despite arguments within the territorial development literature that innovation is an interactive social process and critiques of the linear model of innovation (see Lundvall,

1988; Lundvall, 2007; Lundvall and Johnson, 1994), many social researchers continue to see themselves as outsiders to territorial processes. They analyse the field from the outside, agreeing that there is a theoretical understanding on what should be done, but a lack of knowledge about how to do it. We argue that one of the reasons for this is that much of the literature in the field is abstract and de-contextualised. As a consequence, it obscures the complexity and dilemmas that actors face in territorial development processes. The literature does not show how and why actors become purposive, motivated and enabled to promote change in territories (Sotarauta and Pulkkinen, 2011). We propose action research as an alternative to the analysis of territorial development processes from the outside.

There are two macro trends which our reflections connect with. The first is about the qualitative shift in the last quarter of the twentieth century from an economy based on industry to an economy based on information (Castells, 2000) and theoretical knowledge (Bell, 1974). Castells has labelled this new period 'the Information Age' (Castells, 2000), while Bell (1974) has used the label 'the Knowledge Economy'. The argument from these authors is that the use of information and theoretical knowledge has increased in the economy and is more important than in earlier societies and economies. This trend is challenging universities, research institutes and researchers to engage directly in knowledge creation processes in their territories (Readings, 1996; Nowotny et al., 2001; Slaughter and Leslie, 1997; Slaughter and Rhoades, 2004; Levin, 2007; Pinheiro et al., 2012; Etzkowitz and Leydesdorff, 2001).

The second trend is that more and more policy making, such as innovation policy and territorial development policy, is happening at regional and local levels. At these levels more 'on-the-ground' policy can be developed because there is more information and knowledge about contextual conditions, such as what actors need or lack to increase their competitiveness and potential for development. Policies can be formulated, implemented and monitored in a more targeted way. This creates a challenge for policy makers and territorial actors to continuously learn and redefine policy approaches in order to foster territorial development (Asheim et al., 2007; Boschma and Iammarino, 2009; Cooke and Leydesdorff, 2006; Asheim et al., 2011b; European Commission, 2006; Karlsen et al., 2011; Gustavsen, 2011).

Knowledge is not a stock that can be transferred as an abstract idea and then implemented (Rørvik, 2007). Abstract ideas need to be translated, contextualised and made concrete in order to function. This is a process that takes time, because trust has to be built and because cultural cognitive frameworks take time to change, both for practitioners and researchers. We will argue in this book that these facts and their consequences for territorial development are often overlooked in the literature. This is, in a nutshell, the core of the discussion in the book.

In this book we reflect on micro knowledge creation processes between territorial development actors and researchers facing the challenge of finding actionable solutions in their territories. Our aim is to reflect inside out: the reflections are on processes we have participated in together with territorial actors (elected politicians, civil servants, representatives of development agencies and industry).

The micro processes are connected to the macro trends previously described. Our argument is that by looking closely one may see far – by acquiring a better understanding of micro level territorial development processes and the roles played by individuals and coalitions in them, we may acquire a better understanding of the dynamics of endogenous development processes (Sotarauta et al., 2012). The scarcity of books written from this perspective and our belief that they can be useful in understanding territorial development are the reasons why we are writing this one. However, this is not a 'how to' book. There are no short cuts nor fixed recipes in territorial development. We believe in reflection. Reflection is the foundation for understanding the challenges and problems we face when we participate in processes.

Our Position and Main Argument

We have already stated that our position lies at the intersection between territorial development and action research (Figure I.1). Both fields are much wider than it is possible for us to present and discuss in this book. At the intersection we approach the territorial development literature from the regional innovation system approach. However, we see a need to supplement this analysis with an analysis of knowledge creation processes done inside-out. This is why we use action research. At first glance our position might sound like a contradiction. Territorial development is often analysed as macro processes, and action research is research on micro processes, often in specific organisations, but as we have already argued, micro processes have macro effects in a territory. By studying micro processes one can understand more about the macro effects in a territory.

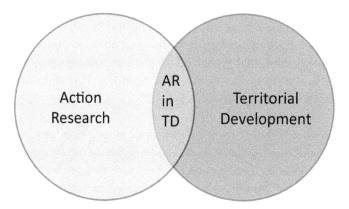

Figure I.1   The intersection between territorial development and action research

At the intersection between these two approaches there is a specific field that can build on action research and the RIS (regional innovation systems) approach, but with its own distinct features. We have called it *action research in territorial development*.

The features of action research in territorial development consist of more than just summing up different concepts from both approaches. We have adopted concepts from these two approaches, combined them and used them in ongoing territorial development processes or new reflections on previous ones. Through this interaction between concepts and experience we have developed new concepts that we present in the following chapters. In this process, the concepts we have adopted have become hybrids. We cannot tell how much of territorial development and how much of action research there is in each of the concepts, but there is certainly a mix in each and every one of them. Later in the book we will present them in more depth.

Reflection Inside Out

The experiences we present in this book are our own experiences from territorial development processes in the Basque Country[1] which go back as far as the mid-1990s. They were not designed in terms of action research from the beginning.

---

1   The precise name for it is the Autonomous Community of the Basque Country, but for simplicity's sake we will use the term 'Basque Country'. This is one of 17 autonomous communities in Spain, with around 2.2 million inhabitants.

As they evolved, the need to have a process perspective on what happened and why it happened grew more and more urgent, and action research provided the framework for this.

By saying that the book is written from the inside out, we mean that our experience of participating in territorial development processes with territorial actors and our reflections on these processes are the foundation for it. Of course, we have not only relied on experience. We all use theories when we interpret our experiences, though they are often tacit. We reflect, but we do not always reflect on why we reflect in a certain way. Our cognitive frameworks (our mental maps) can be tacit for ourselves; they are taken-for-granted assumptions about the world. While cognitive frameworks can be tacit, academic theories are explicit; they are codified in a language that we can understand, and they are universal for all. When we are participating in processes, we use all our knowledge, both tacit knowledge developed from earlier experiences and theoretical knowledge we have acquired. When combining reflection and action, we have tried to reflect on both tacit and theoretical knowledge.

We have organised our experience into case studies, which we present and then discuss in each chapter. Since it is mainly one of us (Miren Larrea) who has lived the cases, the other (James Karlsen) has played the role of the outsider and critically examined the experience-based data used in the cases. This is not the first time we have written about the experiences used in this book, and in Chapter 4 we have integrated these earlier publications. But we have never previously made the effort to present a comprehensive approach in which all elements are put together to show the broad picture of what has happened in terms of research and its contribution to territorial development.

The cases presented in the book are from a local development network, various local development agencies and their association, a research institute and a regional government. The participants in the processes have included about ten researchers and close to a hundred practitioners. Some of the participants have been very involved in the processes, some less so. Some of them, even the practitioners, could give a clear view of what action research is and means for them, whereas some would not even recognise the term. But all were aware of having participated in processes that have resulted in at least mutual knowing and some shared frameworks for territorial development.

The cases have been discussed with the people involved in the stories we tell. We share some of their reactions to the book in the concluding chapter, together with a discussion on validity. The discussion and interpretation of the cases remains our responsibility.

Our Writing Style

The writing style of the book has been a challenge throughout the process. We wanted to look at ourselves from different perspectives and distances. We have tried to reflect this variety of perspectives in our writing, giving the reader the chance to share some of the nuances of each of the positions. The decision to use the first-person plural was taken more than half-way through. It was a result of not finding other styles helpful enough in making experience-based knowledge explicit. We use the first-person plural when we are speaking from our own experience. We have not both been in every situation we describe with the form 'we', but at least one of us was there, and what we write is the result of reflecting together on what happened. We write in the third person when describing what we consider to be facts, and also when we try to establish some distance and connect facts to theory.

This way of writing is inspired by Marshall (2008), who advocates a congruence between form, content and thematic contribution. We come from a background of writing in what Marshall (2008) calls conventional academic scholarship and which she describes as alarmingly impervious to any crises of representation and legitimacy, where much form communicates a deadening and suppression of voice, depersonalisation, acquiescence to norms. We are aware, as she suggests, that well-established conventions favour linear arguments, rationalised discourse, quantitative analysis, value neutrality and so on. That is why finding our own voice to tell this story was one of the hardest challenges when writing this book. We hope we have done it in a way that is fluid for the reader but still helps to share the different angles from which the story is told.

Another of our inspirations in facing this challenge was how Freire (2008b) described his own writing processes. The explicit connection between practice and theory was described by him in his affirmation that: 'It would have been truly impossible to live a process politically so rich, so problem posing, to be so deeply touched by accelerated change, to have participated in so lively discussions.... without all that expressing itself later in one or another theoretical position ...' (Freire, 2008b, p. 58). We were also inspired by his interpretation of his writing process as a critical re-interpretation of his own experience when he says that: 'As a matter of fact I tried to re-understand the plots, the facts, the happenings in which I had participated ... the reading and writing of the word bring a more critical re-reading of the world as a "path" to re-write it, that is, to transform it ...' (Freire, 2008b, p. 62).

It helped us to look for a style that aims at sharing with the reader the connection between the experiences that had been lived and the theory discussed. Freire (2008b) described it by saying that:

> *All that I had started experimenting in Brazil years before, and the knowledge related to it that I had taken with me to the exile, in the memory of my body, was intensely and rigorously lived by me in my years in Chile ... in clarifying readings that made me laugh of happiness, almost like a teenager, when I found in them the theoretical explanation of my practice or the confirmation of the theoretical understanding that my practice had.*
>
> *(Freire, 2008b, p. 63)*

Position and Influences

In this section we briefly present some of the traditions and frameworks we feel have most influenced our reflection and writing process. In doing this we hope to help the reader understand our perspective.

ACTION RESEARCH: INFLUENCES FROM PRAGMATISM AND PAULO FREIRE

We define action research as a research strategy for change in real time where the three elements of research, action and participation are connected and combined in the same process (Greenwood and Levin, 2007).

AR is an umbrella for a diversity of perspectives. There are various classifications of such perspectives. Greenwood and Levin (2007, pp. 133–5) present the following as varieties of action research praxis: pragmatic AR, Southern pragmatic AR, educational strategies, feminist analysis of inequality and development, educational action research, participatory evaluation, participatory rural appraisal, rapid rural appraisal, participatory learning and analysis, human inquiry (collaborative, action, self-reflective and co-operative), action science and organisational learning. They differ in purpose, definitions, epistemologies, ideologies and in the historical context where the research developed.

Other classifications of such approaches are available, for instance by Herr and Anderson (2005, p. 2) and in the *Handbook of Action Research* (Reason and Bradbury, 2008).

The challenge of finding our own place in such a variety is not easy. Conversations with action researchers who apparently shared the same approach let us see that the personal experience of each of them added singularity to their interpretation of what was relevant in AR. Still, we think it is important to be aware of the influences we have received, mainly to be aware of what we take for granted and to develop a self-critical approach to our own praxis. There are two main approaches that have influenced us: pragmatic action research, developed mainly within Norway and Sweden, and the writings of Paulo Freire, which connect us to Latin America.

Pragmatic action research is presented in more depth in Chapters 4, 5 and 6. This approach is influenced by the philosophical tradition of pragmatism. The classical authors within this tradition, which began in the United States in the 1870s, are Charles Sanders Peirce (1905; 1931–58), William James (1978), and especially John Dewey (1916; 1923; Dewey and Bentley, 1975). One of Dewey's most characteristic features was his steadfast refusal to separate thought from action; for him everything was forged in action. For a pragmatist, thinking is also action. When an action is complete and the outcome is different from the expected outcome, a pragmatist starts thinking about why this happened, and through actions tries to find out what caused the outcome. For a pragmatist, action is the only way to generate and test new knowledge (Greenwood and Levin, 2007). The pragmatic tradition claims that the value of knowledge is equal to its practical use.

The pragmatic action research approach was developed in US by Kurt Lewin (1943; 1948) and Chris Argyris and Donald Schön (1974; 1991; 1996). In Norway it has been further developed through the work life research tradition developed by Fred Emery and Einar Thorsrud (1969; 1976), Morten Levin with his American polymath collaborator Davydd Greenwood (Greenwood and Levin, 2007), Bjørn Gustavsen (1992; Toulmin and Gustavsen, 1996), Øyvind Pålshaugen (2004) and Hans Christian Garmann Johnsen (2001), among others. One of us (James Karlsen) was educated through a PhD programme within the work life research tradition where Morten Levin and

Davydd Greenwood were among the teachers. It is because of this strong influence on our research that we have acknowledged the need to make our position clear.

The work of Greenwood, Levin and Gustavsen has to a great extent shaped our language of AR. Their frameworks were the first we used to reflect on our long-term experience working with actors. Concepts like *knowledge cogeneration* (Greenwood and Levin, 2007) and *democratic dialogue* (Gustavsen, 1992) helped us to realise that what we had been doing had some of the features of AR. And it was mostly their language we used to approach actors and propose developing AR processes explicitly for the first time (we will return to these concepts in Chapters 4 and 5).

The second approach that has influenced the way we think about AR and our reflections on this process is that of Paulo Freire (1996; 2008a; 2008b). The context we have been working in throughout the last few years has little to do with the situation in Latin America that inspired Freire's work. Our connection with his contribution and Latin America evolved together with our collaboration with Francisco Alburquerque and Pablo Costamagna which we describe in the following section. Costamagna, who encouraged us to revisit Freire, had been influenced by this author early in his life, and Costamagna later worked on the development of the pedagogical approach to territorial development in Latin America. Our interpretation of Freire is inspired by their praxis on territorial development.

The main influences of Freire on our approach might at first sight look like quite common standpoints. One of them is the recognition of how relevant educational processes are when researchers and territorial actors work together. Until we worked on his concept of pedagogy we had not openly referred to our processes as educational. He poses the need to overcome the contradiction between the teacher and the student by making both researchers and practitioners be simultaneously teachers and students. This, which might sound simple to understand, is very difficult to achieve, as we will argue mainly in Chapters 6 and 7. The rigour with which Freire approaches the method to make this happen is helpful in being aware of such difficulties and facing them. The other critical contribution from Freire that has influenced us and shaped Chapter 7 is the impossibility of the researcher being neutral and the discussion of his or her political role. In this case what we get from Freire is not a carefully designed method, but a deep reflection on the responsibility of researchers to assume their political role.

INFLUENCES ON TERRITORIAL DEVELOPMENT

The starting point for this book is within the territorial development literature that emphasises learning and innovation as important endogenous factors for development, such as the Nordic School of the learning economy (Isaksen, 2001). It highlights innovation as the basis for achieving competitiveness by firms, regions and nations. Innovation is conceptualised as a complex, interactive, non-linear learning process. Compared to neoclassical regional growth models, these territorial innovation models share the view that learning and innovation will improve the market-economic performance of a territory. This approach has been developed, among others, by Nordic evolutionary economists and economic geographers such as Lundvall (1992; 2007; Lundvall and Johnson, 1994), Asheim (1996; 2001; Asheim and Isaksen, 2002; Asheim and Gertler, 2005; Asheim and Hansen, 2009; Asheim et al., 2011a; Asheim et al., 2011b), Edquist (1997; 2005) and Isaksen (2007; 2009; Isaksen and Kalsaas, 2009).

One of us (James Karlsen) has been working on the RIS concept mainly with Arne Isaksen for the last few years, which has been the departure point for our reflections on territorial development in this book. The RIS concept is presented in Chapter 1, so we will not discuss it extensively here. Instead we will focus on what we feel is Isaksen's contribution to our understanding of territorial development, and especially the RIS approach. We have studied both clusters and single firms in different regions of Norway (Isaksen and Karlsen, 2010; Isaksen and Karlsen, 2012a; Isaksen and Karlsen, 2012b; Isaksen and Karlsen, 2013). One common factor in these studies is the systemic perspective, which implies that firms are connected to other actors both in their host territory and abroad. The relationship with other actors is important for innovation processes in firms, in clusters and for territorial development. There is 'something that matters' for firms' innovation processes that is not only localised within the single firm but in the connection to a local, regional and even national innovation system. It relates to what Marshall (1890) called 'industrial atmosphere'. Our approach is that there is 'something' in the social relationship between actors – people matters in innovation processes. This 'something' is what we explore further in this book.

Another contribution that has shaped our understanding of territorial development, and is deeply connected to the concept of industrial atmosphere, is the literature on industrial districts. This was the main framework for one of us (Miren Larrea) when introduced to research through the PhD process. Marshall (1890) defined an industrial district as a complex and intractable network of external economies and diseconomies, of connections in costs and historical and cultural factors that include inter-firm relations as well as inter-personal ones. For Becattini (1979), territory is not a mere framework of economy, but an economic resource. That is why, he says, the quality of territory is what makes it possible for technology to cross with a determined culture, for firms to find specific environments, for markets to translate competition into co-operation, and for the economy to mobilise society and the interactions of each if its members. Economic thinking that omits the territorial dimension loses the link that makes these connections possible. Territory therefore matters in economic processes, and it matters in times of change. One of the practical influences of these contributions is the relevance of local economic development in our approach to territorial development. As we will explain later in this chapter, by local we mean supra-municipal but sub-regional processes for development.

Another influence that is not dealt with in the book in an explicit way but which underlies the cases is the influence of competitiveness literature based on the contributions of Porter (1990). It has been one of the approaches used to work with practitioners in some of the projects described throughout the book. It has thus been used more in the dialogue with territorial actors than in the later process of reflecting and writing this book.

Finally, in the later years of the process we reflect on, we have been influenced by two authors who have worked mainly in Latin America and whom we have already mentioned when referring to our connection to Freire. They are Alburquerque and Costamagna (Alburquerque, 2000; Costamagna and Saltarelli, 2004; Costamagna, 2006; Alburquerque et al., 2008; Alburquerque, 2012). Part of their influence is related to their trajectory in ECLAC (the Economic Commission for Latin America and the Caribbean) and has taken place as we have been invited to share our reflections and learning process in ConectaDEL, a training programme for territorial development linked to MIF (Multilateral Investment Fund) a member of IDB (Inter-American Development Bank). But, as mentioned earlier, what has influenced us most is their praxis, materialised into ongoing dialogue with a multiplicity of actors working on territorial development in a wide array of countries in Latin America. These authors define local economic development as a process of accumulation of capabilities with the aim of improving the economic wellbeing of a community in a collective and ongoing way. This capability for development refers as much to the circumstances of the territorial economy as to those of its socioeconomic actors and institutions. They advocate a management of these processes that is consensus-oriented and participatory, and emphasise the need to construct territorial capabilities for action (Alburquerque et al., 2008, pp. 16–21). The definitions of territory and territorial development we give in the following section are also part of their influence on this book.

Main Concepts Used Throughout the Book

When approaching each discussion, we will define the new concepts we introduce. But there are some basic concepts we want to introduce at the beginning, either because they are important throughout the book or because they might confuse the reader unless our meaning is made clear from the start. These concepts are territory, territorial development, action research, territorial actors, political actors, policy makers and agora.

TERRITORY AND DEVELOPMENT

The territorial level that is relevant for the regional innovation system approach is the region. We use the definition of region given by Cooke et al. (2007) when they say that the region can be defined as a political unit of medium level, between the national or federal and local levels of government, with a certain cultural homogeneity. From this perspective, regional development is a process that has the wellbeing of the inhabitants of a region as its final aim. Innovation is considered the main means for development. That is why there is a strong focus on innovation policy. This perspective is mainly related to economic development and is our point of departure on *what* territorial development is in this book.

When we integrate action research with territorial development, the process perspective becomes critical and poses the question of *how* territorial development happens. A definition of territory that fits with the process perspective is given by Alburquerque (2012), who defines territory as the actors who live in a place with their social, economic and political organisation, their culture and institutions as well as the physical environment they are part of. This definition gives a central position to actors and does not necessarily refer to any single territorial level – it does not exclusively refer to the municipal, local or regional level. From this perspective, he defines territorial development as the process of mobilisation and participation of different actors (public and private) in which they discuss and agree on the strategies that can guide individual as well as collective behaviour.

These two approaches to the *what* and the *how* of territorial development are complementary and are intertwined when we use the concepts of territory and territorial development throughout the book.

The book departs from the perspective of territorial development proposed by the regional innovation system literature. We are aware that this literature uses the term 'regional development' much more than 'territorial development'. We have decided to use the term 'territorial' instead of 'regional' (or 'local') in order to emphasise on the one hand that our contributions are the result of reflecting on different territorial levels inside a region (region, province, county, municipality) and on the other hand that development requires a multi-level approach, which means that the connections between levels must also be understood. We consider that the concepts and frameworks we use are not applicable at the national level, and that is why we have not included it in the multiple territorial levels analysed in the book. But the influence of national policy on the rest of levels is understood as part of the multi-level approach.

In the book we will analyse processes that have taken place at county, provincial and regional levels in the Basque Country. When we use these concepts in the book, we refer to political units where a specific government or agency has its area of influence. Thus, when we refer to a single municipality, we will talk about the municipal level. For us, local level means a supra-municipal but sub-regional level. In the book this is represented by counties, which have no government but do have county development agencies supported by various municipalities that together form the agency. Next there are provinces. The provinces have their own governments and parliaments directly elected by citizens. Finally, we use the term 'region' to refer to the whole Basque Country.

The result is a dense institutional framework, with four different administrative levels affecting innovation policy. The Spanish government has a mainly regulatory role; the Basque Government has substantial autonomy to define industrial policy and is well known for its strong, proactive industrial policies over the last three decades. The provincial councils play a critical role, as they are in charge of collecting taxes and they define innovation policy. Finally, municipal authorities (especially in the larger cities) and the local development agencies promoted by them have substantial capacity to reach the final beneficiaries of such policies (Aranguren et al., 2012a).

Figure I.2   Map of the Autonomous Community of the Basque Country
Source: A. Murciego, Orkestra.

Figure I.2 is a map of the Basque Country on which we locate the case studies that are used in the different parts of the book. Part I of the book is based on the case of Ezagutza Gunea (EG), a county development network in Urola Erdia County, which consists of two municipalities, Azkoitia and Azpeitia. It is the darkest area in the centre of the map. Part II of the book is based on the case of Orkestra, which has the whole region of the Basque Country as its area of influence. This area is divided into three provinces: Bizkaia, Gipuzkoa and Alava. Gipuzkoa is shaded darker as it is the area of influence of Gipuzkoa Sarean, the project launched by the Provincial Council of Gipuzkoa that is used as the case for Part III.

AGORA: THE SPACE WHERE RESEARCHERS AND TERRITORIAL ACTORS MEET

The agora is one of the main concepts in this book, the one that maintains the thread throughout the chapters. In its most general sense, an agora is a common space where different actors meet. We take a more specific approach to the agora. It is the public space in which 'science meets the public' and in which the public 'speaks back to science'. It is the domain (in fact, many domains) in which contextualisation occurs and in which socially robust knowledge is continually subjected to testing while becoming more robust in the process. Neither state nor market, neither exclusively private nor exclusively public, the agora is a space in which societal and scientific problems are framed and defined and where what will ultimately be accepted as a 'solution' is negotiated (Nowotny et al., 2001, p. 247).

We use the concept of agora as a space, interpreting space as relational. This means that space is generated by interactions and interrelations. In doing so, we agree with Murdoch (2006) when he writes that space is both *consensual* and *contested* – consensual because relations are usually made out of agreements or alignments between two or more entities; contested because the construction of one set of relations may involve both the exclusion of some entities and the forcible enrolment of others. Murdoch (2006) describes a relational space as a power-filled space in which some alignments come to dominate, at least for a certain period, while others come to be dominated.

The concrete cases we present focus the agora mostly in the interactions between researchers and a specific type of actor in territories: policy makers (see the definition below).

We had discussions on whether the agora should be defined as a space or a process. Our argument is that an agora is a space. Throughout the book, and particularly in Chapters 6 and 7, we will further develop the concept of dialogue, which we consider to be the process continuously going on in the agora. The agora as a space is shaped by the dialogue.

TERRITORIAL ACTORS, POLITICAL ACTORS AND POLICY MAKERS

We have underlined that our approach to territorial development is focused on actors. There is no territorial development without actors. From our point of view, territorial actors can be organisations as well as individuals. Usually in territorial development processes it is mainly organisations that are considered: a government, a development agency, a firm, a training centre, a technology centre, a university. But the ones participating in meetings and conversations, keeping the dialogue alive and developing trust, are specific individuals. Their roles, the decisions they make, how they speak and behave are influenced both by their personal approach and by the organisation they come from. There is not always a perfect alignment between the organisational goals and the goals of the person representing them. As a matter of fact, organisations are complex and there is a multiplicity of perspectives in them that a single person can hardly represent.

Throughout the book we acknowledge the relevance of both organisations and individuals. When analysing the behaviour of individuals in cases we will portray them as guided by emotions, and not only by rational thinking. Individuals who get involved in situations of conflict and power play are influenced by ideology and have different senses of belonging, fears, dreams and expectations. These are aspects that are lacking in most frameworks for territorial development, yet greatly influence territorial development.

Throughout the text we will also talk about political actors. When we do so, we are not exclusively talking about elected politicians or members of governments. We define 'political' as *relating to the individual's views about social relationships involving authority or power*. What we mean by this is that any individual actor in the territory either representing himself or herself or any public or private organisation has a view on what the desirable state of social relationships would be and often acts in order to develop such a view. This is the way we use the term 'political actor', and we do not relate it to partisan interest but to the legitimate contribution of any individual or organisation to the construction of the territory. In this sense, there are political actors not only in governments and their agencies, but also in firms, universities, technology centres, training centres and so on.

When we refer to those individuals representing governments and their agencies we will use other terms. Sometimes we will distinguish between elected politicians, those who participate in elections and have the responsibility to govern, and civil servants who remain in the different governments and agencies independent of the political cycles. When we use the term 'policy makers', we apply the definition *persons responsible for making policy, especially in governments*, referring to both elected politicians and civil servants.

Finally, we will sometimes use the term 'practitioners', usually when we are reflecting on the different roles of researchers and practitioners in an action research process. With this term we refer to those who approach action research from practice. It has a wider scope than the term 'policy makers'. In the cases analysed in the book, most practitioners are policy makers, but there are also company representatives, representatives from universities, training centres, technology centres and so on.

CHANGE

There are different approaches to change. From a general approach it can be interpreted as disequilibrium – as an imbalance in the process from one point of equilibrium towards another point of equilibrium. Change in this case is abrupt, temporary and a distortion of a balance. When the new balance is established, the change process is over. This approach is based on Kurt Lewin's notion of change as a three-phase sequence of events: (1) melt the old, (2) make change and (3) freeze the new (Sotarauta and Pulkkinen, 2011). From this point of view, change is seen as a discontinuous period between periods of stability and continuity.

Change can also be interpreted as a very slow and creeping process where there is no equilibrium to reach. In this approach, change is not an exceptional and one-time process, but the normal state of things. From this perspective, change can only be studied in the long term.

Change has many names, such as territorial development, innovation, economic growth, economic crisis, reforms and so on. At the macro level there are a lot of indicators for measuring change from one period to another, such as population, unemployment, profit within an industry, rate of innovation and so on. But when it comes to micro processes and change is embodied in the behaviour of specific actors of flesh and bone, it can be difficult to measure. Although the title of this book is not explicit about it, we are reflecting on long-term policy processes with a limited number of participants. From this perspective, change is an ongoing, incremental and slow process – so slow and incremental that as participants in a process, we have not always been aware of it. It can be hard to detect what it was that caused a change and when it happened. The approach to change in the book is based on reflecting on experience to detect and understand change at the micro level. We then try to create the concepts and frameworks to help others to reflect on their own experiences.

REFLECTION IN AND ON ACTION

Schön (1983) distinguishes between two types of reflection: reflection-in-action and reflection-on-action. The former is the kind of reflection we do when we are acting.

Reflection-in-action is a conscious activity. If something is not working correctly (does not seem right), then you reflect when you are doing the action. In action we have the possibility of changing the action through thinking.

Reflection-on-action is thinking about actions after a process and the transformation of this to a written text, such as an academic article or a book. As Schön (1983, p. 26) says: 'We reflect on action, thinking back on what we have done in order to discover how our knowing-in-action may have contributed to an unexpected outcome.'

In this book we combine reflection-in-action and reflection-on-action.

Contents and Structure of the Book

The book is divided into three parts. Part I focuses on the approach to territorial development that has most influenced us, which is that of regional innovation systems. We point out in Chapter 1 that this literature has focused mostly on technological and organisational innovation. We argue for a complementary approach between technological and social innovation in order to generate territorial development. It is in the development of this approach to social innovation in agoras for territorial development that we see a critical role for social researchers. In Chapter 2 we argue that agoras are naturally spaces in conflict and we share some concepts and frameworks that help develop awareness of this conflict. In Chapter 3 we propose the generation of collective knowing as the path for managing conflict and reaching consensus for action. Throughout Part I the case of Ezagutza Gunea, a public–private co-operation network for county development, is presented as the experience at the base of our reflection process.

Part II enters the discussion of what we see when we try to open the black box of agoras for territorial development. We argue in Chapter 4 that agoras follow principles described as Mode 2 knowledge generation – knowledge generation in the context of application. We also argue that action research contributes with frameworks that help us to understand what goes on in Mode 2 knowledge generation processes in social research. In Chapter 5 we discuss how environments for action research can be developed to help the construction of agoras for territorial development. In both chapters we reflect on our experience in constructing an environment for AR in Orkestra, the Basque Institute of Competitiveness.

Finally, Part III focuses on dialogue, the critical process going on in the agoras for territorial development. Based on the thinking of two authors, we see dialogue as a process that can generate deep social change. The first, analysed in Chapter 6, is Bjørn Gustavsen. Using his concept of democratic dialogue we reflect on the relationship between researchers and policy makers in the agora and how the status of the participants shapes research and action. The second is Paulo Freire, whose contribution we use in Chapter 7. His pedagogical approach helps us to reflect on how different spaces for dialogue can be constructed in territorial development processes and how relevant it is to have an awareness of the ideological position of researchers and practitioners when learning together.

The final chapter of the book approaches the challenge of testing its validity, and in doing so we present the concept of *connectivity*, which proposes going beyond transferability of the concepts to try to integrate them into new development processes.

PART I

Social Innovation, Conflict and Collective Knowing

Our argument throughout Part I is that social researchers have a role in generating social innovation for territorial development (Chapter 1). To fulfil this role, they must work together with other territorial actors in agoras, which are naturally spaces in conflict (Chapter 2). The way out of conflict into action is the construction of collective knowing (Chapter 3).

When we have discussed our framework with colleagues, social innovation has been the most provocative concept. We have been asked about the definition of *social innovation*, whereas with the concept of *innovation*, nobody ever demanded a definition. There may be different explanations for this reaction. It might simply be that the concept of social innovation is relatively new and therefore needs some time before it is accepted, while an 'official' and widely accepted definition of innovation exists. Acceptance of new concepts is a social process; it takes time. It may also be that it touches some deeper, taken-for-granted assumption about innovation – that social innovation is not among the relevant issues in regional innovation systems. It is not our intention to explore this reaction further, but to share our awareness that the concepts we are using in this part of the book are not very widely used within the regional innovation systems literature. Our aim in using them is not to provoke, but to develop the framework further so that it will be more workable in territorial development processes.

Why these three concepts (social innovation, conflict and collective knowing)? Our argument for using them is not first and foremost that they enhance understanding of territorial development processes from a theoretical approach. Rather, it is because we have seen them as important and useful in our practice as researchers in territorial development processes with practitioners. The common core of the concepts is that they acknowledge and integrate the social aspect. Innovation is basically a social process, as are conflict and collective knowing. Conflict is as natural as consensus, but this is seldom reflected within the territorial development literature. Collective knowing is the social process of creating a common ground for action and for acting in alignment with others. This concept is probably the least known of the three, but when taken into action it has a great potential for macro changes.

In this part we do not yet use the concept of action research, which we will introduce in Part II. We argue in terms of the role of social researchers knowing that there are different approaches to playing this role, and action research is one of them. The research we have done throughout the years in EG – the case study the three chapters share – combines participatory processes, research and action from the beginning in 2002, but has an explicit approach to action research only after 2007. Part I mainly focuses in change processes of territorial actors when they interact with social researchers. The change processes of researchers in the same types of situations will be addressed in Part II.

Regional Innovation Systems from the Inside Out

For a seminar in Norway, a researcher was invited to present his analysis of the region. During his presentation he showed a slide containing many dots which he called 'lumps'. In the next slide he showed arrows between the dots. From 'lump to cluster', he said, 'the core is to create interactions. … Everything is about being connected.' He concluded the presentation by offering some policy recommendations for creating interaction between universities and industry. However, we were working in the region at that time and felt that the presentation left some unanswered questions in terms of *how* to create connectedness. It seemed very easy on paper, but we knew that it was not.

This brief account shows how differently the same phenomenon can be perceived depending on one's perspective. For instance, take the phenomenon of lack of interaction between actors. The researcher's perspective was from the *outside in*, whereas we, as participants in the process of creating interaction, saw it from a different perspective: we were looking at it *inside out*.

As researchers, we have carried out outside-in analysis. However, we argue that this type of analysis does not capture many of the processes inside a regional innovation system (RIS) – a substantial part of what is really happening. As we argued in the Introduction, most training and concepts related to RISs are oriented towards conducting outside-in analysis, as opposed to reflecting on processes in which researchers themselves participate. Researchers do not necessarily see themselves as participants in the system. In this chapter we look more deeply at this idea. We argue that our (that is, social researchers') own interactions with other researchers and practitioners (companies and policy making organisations) are part of the interactions that need to be constructed in a territorial development process. Although this is not a new approach, for us it constitutes a new perspective on analysing and understanding processes in which we have been participating. To us, looking at the RIS *inside out* means that we know that we are another actor in the system. We will argue that traditional approaches to territorial innovation models create a partial perspective, leading social researchers to play the role of outside observers and analysts.

In this chapter we begin with a discussion of the frameworks that have influenced our understanding of RISs. We will use the concept of 'agora' presented in the Introduction and argue that agoras are not only spaces to facilitate technological innovation, but are essentially spaces for social innovation. We argue that social researchers can have a role in the creation of the social innovation which is required in order to make technological and organisational innovation happen in an RIS. This can be understood as the role of social researchers in micro processes in an RIS, which is the focus for our inside-out approach.

The chapter is structured so that the main concepts that will be used in the discussion are presented first. We write briefly about RISs and our approach to social innovation. This concept has been used very loosely, and we propose an approach that can help explain the role of social researchers in the agora without opening up a major debate on the concept itself. Then we advocate a more explicit place for social researchers and their interactions with other actors in the most influential RIS frameworks. In order to discuss this contribution from not only the conceptual perspective but also from experience, we use the case of Ezagutza Gunea (EG). EG is a county network for public–private co-operation that reflects the conceptualisation of micro processes in RISs which we focus on. By discussing this case we develop our main arguments about the role of social innovation in the agora and the links between social and technological innovation.

Regional Innovation Systems

RIS is a theoretical concept put forth by Cooke (1992; 1998) that has increased in popularity in recent decades, both among researchers and practitioners addressing policy making issues on different geographical levels (Asheim et al., 2011b). According to Asheim et al., the concept is a generic framework that combines a range of different factors in a region that promote and diffuse innovation. Our goal is not to carry out a literature review on what has been said about the concept, but to concentrate on how some influential frameworks have been interpreted by many researchers in the field (ourselves included) in a way that might have hindered our active role within it.

An RIS is an 'institutional and organisational infrastructure interacting and supporting innovation within the production system of a region' (Asheim, 2011, p. 111). The main focus for the RIS approach is to understand and explain the region as an economic system for knowledge creation and regional development and give policy recommendations. An innovation system is usually interpreted as the interaction between 'private and public firms (either large or small), universities and government agencies aiming at the production of science and technology' (Niosi et al., 1993, p. 212).

An RIS is usually described as consisting of two subsystems: the knowledge application and exploitation subsystem (production subsystem) and the knowledge exploration and diffusion subsystem (knowledge subsystem) (see Figure 1.1 later in this chapter).

The production subsystem can consist of one or several clusters. A regional cluster is an agglomeration of firms that are related to each other in some way, such as through supplier or customer relations or by being competitors. The competitive advantage of a cluster is shaped by competition and collaboration between firms and other actors in the cluster (Porter, 1998).

The knowledge subsystem can be narrow or broad in scope. The narrow definition includes mainly R&D activities carried out by universities, research institutes and firms' R&D departments. The broader definition includes all actors and activities connected with learning, education of the workforce and training of a skilled workforce. The broader definition also acknowledges that the university can have an important role in educating well-qualified workers for the labour market and that training centres are important for the education and upgrading of skilled workers (Lundvall, 2007, p. 97).

However, the concept of the RIS includes not only the subsystems, but also the critical element of the interactions between them. According to Trippl and Tödtling (2007), the existence of intensive interactions and knowledge flows between the RIS subsystems, leading to regional collective learning and systemic innovation, is considered to be a central feature of highly innovative regions. Socio-institutional factors are important for understanding these interactions. The common habits, routines, practices and rules prevailing in an area –

that is, the socio-institutional and cultural setting specific to a region – greatly influence its innovation capacity, as they regulate the interactions between the innovation actors (Johnson, 1992; Gertler, 2004; Edquist, 2005). Consequently, institutional factors such as the dominant patterns of behaviour, the culture of co-operation and even attitudes towards innovation and technological progress constitute important RIS elements.

The RIS approach highlights the importance of interaction and learning among companies and between companies and knowledge organisations in a region for creating innovations (Asheim and Gertler, 2005). These are the micro foundations of an innovation system, which must be connected to a macro perspective. An innovation process is a complex interplay between micro and macro, where macro structures create conditions for micro processes, and micro processes influence macro structures (Lundvall, 2007). As mentioned above, Part I of the book focuses on micro perspectives, while its connections to macro change will be discussed in Part III.

The latest developments in the RIS field show a trend towards a dynamic perspective on the creation of interactions. One of the RIS-related concepts that integrates this perspective is that of *constructing regional advantage* and its approach to public–private partnership (Asheim et al., 2007; Asheim et al., 2011a; Karlsen et al., 2011). This proposes that policy can play a role in a dynamic perspective on constructing regional advantages. This approach focuses on the role and impact of the public sector in the economy and emphasises policy support, particularly in public–private partnerships. Another related perspective is the SMART (Specific, Measurable, Attainable, Realistic and Timely) specialisation literature, which develops a process perspective in which interactions become critical (Foray, 2009; Foray et al., 2009; Foray et al., 2011; European Commission, 2012; Navarro and Magro, 2013). Despite the strong arguments for interactions and the development of policy tools to create them, interactions in regional innovation systems remain a challenge in many territories.

What are We Lacking in the RIS Approach?

The RIS literature has underlined that innovation is a social process (Cooke et al., 2000; Lundvall and Johnson, 1994). Our argument is that when implementing policies, this aspect has been underestimated and there is a need to further understand how to intervene on the social side of innovation processes.

Our main argument is that there is a place for social researchers within the RIS approach that has not been discussed by the proponents of the approach. We believe social researchers have a natural role in RISs through their participation in agoras. But the mainstream approach to RISs has given a central role to researchers in the technological field as drivers of technological innovation, and has not placed the same emphasis on the role of social researchers as drivers of social innovation. There are many possible reasons for this. We believe one reason is that RISs have been conceptualised in a way that gives a central role to technological innovation and, consequently, to researchers in the science and technology fields. As a result, the role of social researchers in RISs has been understood narrowly, without considering all the roles they could have played.

Social innovation has hardly been considered as part of RISs. We advocate an understanding of the social researcher as an active change agent in RISs – contributing to social innovation in the micro processes between actors in the system. We will develop this argument further in the following sections.

WE LACK A MORE EXPLICIT APPROACH TO SOCIAL INNOVATION

We are aware that the multiple approaches to and definitions of social innovation have made many researchers in the RIS field reluctant to use the concept. Hence, we will use this section to clarify our own approach to the term.

Moulaert and Nussbaumer (2005) opened the debate on a broader meaning of the term 'innovation' and its significance for local and regional development. They take social innovation as a key concept and consider it as a twin term to technological innovation. They say that the concept is twofold: first, it refers to the satisfaction of basic human needs; this is the meaning adopted in the social economy and in alternative development literature. Moulaert and Nussbaumer (2005) relate the concept to markets by saying provocatively that the more egalitarian the market economy, the better the market mechanisms will work as an allocation mechanism for satisfying basic needs. But the approach mainly focuses on needs that markets do not respond to. Second, regarding its twofold character, social innovation also refers to innovation in social relations between individuals and groups of humans in communities. Among these relationships, they include those existing within and among ethnic groups, as well as professional relationships, labour relationships, market relationships and governance relationships.

When we talk about social innovation in the RIS in this book, we define it as innovation in the way the actors in the RIS relate to each other (to implement new patterns for interaction among actors that generate value is social innovation). It responds to the second definition of Moulaert and Nussbaumer (2005) in their twofold approach. So why use the term 'social innovation' instead of just talking about innovation in social relationships in the RIS?

The experiences we discuss throughout this book make us advocate the use of the term 'social innovation' in RISs because, although we focus on the second of Moulaert and Nussbaumer's definitions (Moulaert and Nussbaumer, 2005), we believe that they are both linked. It is difficult to argue for change in the way actors relate to each other in RISs and think that this is independent from wider changes in society. We believe this is a relevant issue in terms of the changes that agoras can create in territorial development: by developing new modes of interaction in the context of market-oriented innovation in RISs, new governance modes emerge that are linked to deeper social change. Our approach to this wider perspective on social change will be considered in Part III, but by presenting the connection here, we want to say that even the more restrictive approaches to social innovation are linked to complex social changes. Still, from a practical point of view, we only refer to the second definition when using the concept of 'social innovation' in this book.

In our approach to social innovation in RISs, social and technological innovation are complementary. Moulaert and Nussbaumer (2005) criticise the fact that although the literature on territorial innovation models has discussed both technological and social innovation, social innovation is assumed to be instrumental in technological innovation and competitiveness. Although they are not explicit about it, we think this can be applied to both of their definitions of social innovation. We do not want the preponderance of one type of innovation or another to become the central discussion of this book. Instead, we will elaborate on the complementary character of both.

Finally, from the agora perspective, the social innovation approach helps us to argue that, just as researchers in technological fields interact with actors in the different subsystems to stimulate innovation in new products, processes, materials and so on, social researchers can also interact to innovate in new modes of relationships within the system. They can do so not only by analysing the system from the outside, but by participating in the construction of such modes. Social innovation processes start when individuals change their consciousness and apply this within their community or particular group to transform the territory or society (Chombart de Lauwe, 1976). Social researchers can support processes to bring about such a change of conscience and subsequently apply it in territorial processes.

The assumption that, along with technological innovation, social innovation is a relevant concept in RISs calls for a more explicit role for social researchers in the knowledge generation and diffusion subsystem of RISs. No definition in this literature lets them off the hook, and many have played a role in the *analysis* of social innovation. Still, there is little literature that makes their role explicit in the *construction* of social innovation.

WE LACK AN ACTIVE ROLE FOR SOCIAL RESEARCHERS INSIDE THE SYSTEM

One of the most frequently used illustrations of an RIS is from Tödtling and Trippl (2005). In a later publication, the same authors offer another illustration of an RIS (Trippl and Tödtling, 2007). We believe these two illustrations of RISs demonstrate the idea that 'there appear to be as many, explicit or implicit, "ideal models" of RISs as there are policy applications' (De Bruijn and Lagendijk, 2005, p. 1,155). We see this as a consequence of the increased interest in the RIS approach. The RIS approach is used more and more, but is still under-theorised (Asheim et al., 2011b). It also illustrates that the more a concept is used, the greater the chances of different interpretations of the concept emerging.[1] Ours is one such interpretation and contribution to the generic approach to RISs. We will use the two illustrations to discuss what we mean is lacking in the RIS approach, and consequently, what this book aims to contribute. Our arguments are meant as a constructive critique of RISs with the aim of developing the concept further.

The first part of our argument is that the influential article and Figure 1.1 illustrating RISs by Tödtling and Trippl (2005) affected the way we perceived the role of the social researcher.[2] The authors argue that policy tools are important for stimulating innovation processes and interactions between the subsystems. Their argument is that 'policy actors at this level can play a powerful role in shaping regional innovation processes, provided that there is sufficient regional autonomy (legal competencies and financial resources)

---

1   This is not unique to RISs, but has also happened to the cluster concept developed by Porter (1998); see, for example, Martin and Sunley (2003) for a discussion of the cluster concept.
2   Another influential framework is the triple helix (Etzkowitz and Leydesdorff, 2001). We believe that despite being more explicit and direct about the role of government and the public sector (Asheim, 2011), it also lacks an explicit approach to social research. We have adopted the RIS approach to develop our argument because it has more clearly influenced the experience from which we write.

to formulate and implement innovation policies' (Tödtling and Trippl, 2005, p. 1,206). We agree with this, but would also like to add a different perspective.

Figure 1.1 indicates that the role of policy makers is to find the right policy tools and apply them in the system. The unidirectional arrows from policy makers to the other subsystems could be interpreted in this way, and we have often found this interpretation among researchers and policy makers. In this respect, the RIS approach has already been criticised for interpreting policy making as a mechanical stimulus–response model or a black box (Uyarra, 2010). The arrows in Figure 1.1 show policy as an element that can stimulate processes, but cannot be influenced by them. Consequently, social researchers conceiving themselves in the knowledge production subsystem and studying the policy process would be positioned 'outside' the policy process, potentially influenced by policy tools, but not interacting with policy makers.

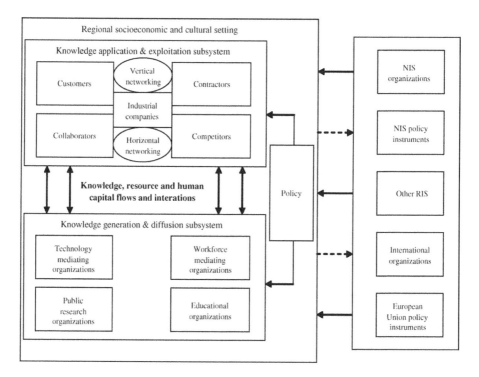

Figure 1.1   The main structure of regional innovation systems

Note: NIS = national innovation system.
Source: Adapted from Tödtling, F. and Trippl, M. (2005) 'One Size Fits All? Towards a Differentiated Regional Innovation Policy Approach'. *Research Policy* 34: 1,203–19. Reproduced with permission from Elsevier.

We are aware that there has been interaction between researchers and policy makers when defining policy tools. Our argument is that social researchers have been engaged mainly as outsiders, as analysts giving recommendations to policy makers, and not as actors in these processes.

To make a different role of social researchers more visible in RISs, we propose to work with a less influential diagram produced by Trippl and Tödtling (2007). In this article, the authors argue that government organisations and regional development agencies constitute a third RIS subsystem that deserves closer attention when it comes to innovation policy. The role of the sub-national policy level in encouraging a region's development has been underlined by others too (Cooke et al., 2000; Asheim et al., 2003; Tödtling and Trippl, 2005) (see Figure 1.2).

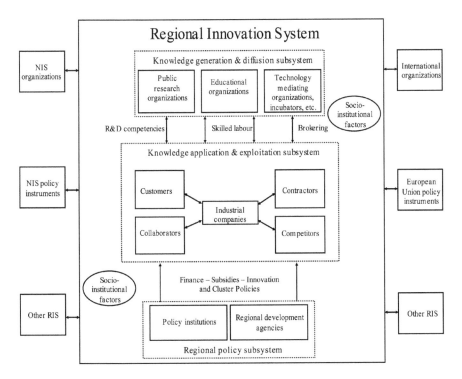

Figure 1.2   The main structuring of regional innovation systems

Source: Adapted from Trippl, M. and Tödtling, F. (2007) 'Developing Biotechnology Clusters in Non-high Technology Regions: The Case of Austria'. *Industry and Innovation* 14, p. 49. Reproduced by permission of the publisher, Taylor & Francis Ltd, http://www.tandf.co.uk/journals.

We consider this argument from Trippl and Tödtling (2007) a step towards increased understanding of one of the roles of social researchers in RISs, as it gives policy the status of a subsystem, making governments and agencies more visible as relevant actors. Still, the relationships that are drawn from them are only connected to the production subsystem and not the knowledge subsystem, and they remain unidirectional. This means that the bidirectional relationship between the knowledge generation and diffusion subsystem and the regional policy subsystem, which could facilitate a mutual learning process between policy makers and social researchers, is still not there.

Our proposal is to complement the two diagrams that have shaped our understanding of our own role in the RIS with an explicit role for social researchers who, as part of the knowledge subsystem, interact with policy makers in the policy subsystem in a mutually shaping relationship. That is, we propose to be more explicit when considering policy learning with the participation of social researchers as a natural process in RISs.

The Micro Perspective

In order to position agoras and social researchers in RISs, we return to the argument given by Lundvall (2007) in terms of micro and macro processes. We think that the traditional figures of RISs that represent the subsystems help us think in terms of the macro perspective on RISs. Figures 1.1 and 1.2 explain RISs in terms of interactions between subsystems, but interaction between subsystems is an abstraction. It is people – usually representing organisations – that interact in RISs. We know this is implicit in the framework, but it must be made explicit to locate the agora in RISs and the place of social researchers in that agora. Otherwise, there could be a risk of approaching RISs from a sector perspective, describing what elements are present in each of the subsystems, but with very little understanding of how interactions unfold. The reason why we focus in the micro perspective is related to our decision to write this book inside out, departing from concrete experiences. This perspective is not enough by itself, and is complementary to the macro perspective of RISs that helps us to understand the structural elements of RISs that heavily influence micro processes.

RISs have already been conceptualised as networks. For instance, Asheim and Coenen (2006) argue that innovations are carried out through networks of various actors underpinned by an institutional framework. Thus, innovation systems are viewed as interaction networks (Edquist, 1997; Kaufmann and Tödtling, 2000). Lorentzen (2008) argues that innovation spaces are socially constructed through the creation of knowledge networks on a variety of scales. This means that RISs could be represented as actors in a networked structure of interrelationships, as shown in Figure 1.3. Some of the small circles in the lower diagram are illustrations of social researchers.

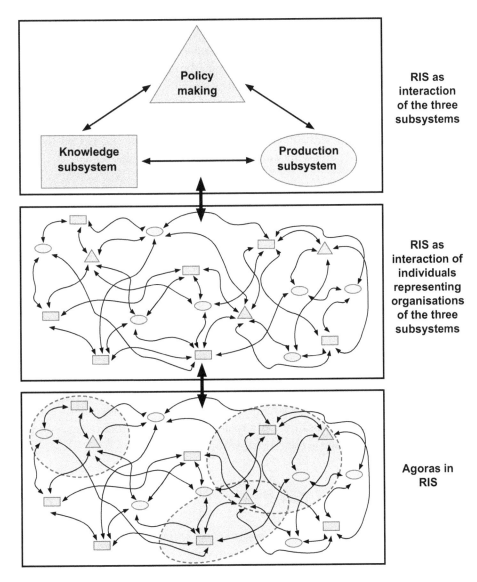

Figure 1.3   An approach to the agora in RISs

Source: Adapted from Karlsen and Larrea (2012a), p. 215.

From our perspective, this networked structure would be an alternative way to represent an RIS. But representing an RIS as one homogeneous network can also create bias. There are spaces in territories where such networked interactions generate cycles of reflection and action. When researchers participate in such processes, we will argue that these spaces are agoras. From now on, we will focus on one specific type of agora – those where territorial actors and social researchers interact in the context of policy processes for territorial development.

The moment we, social researchers, perceive ourselves as one more actor in the network and not someone observing from the outside, we are aware of whom the other actors we interact with are. The connections that we have with actors in the other subsystems can influence the process of territorial development. The arrows are, of course, bidirectional. The researchers that engage in interactions with other actors in the RIS can be influenced by the other actors' ways of perceiving and acting upon the system.

Once focused on their specific network of interactions, researchers are aware that the interactions are far from rational, maximising relationships. They are led by concrete individuals who have different motivations, get involved in power play and have different mental frameworks. Understanding what causes change is not about reaching the theoretically perfect answer. Instead, it is necessary to understand the essence of power play, trust, leadership, emotions and so on. It is not exclusively about the right economics, economic geography or industrial economic approaches. The involvement of researchers in an RIS is not only a matter of rational frameworks and concepts, but also an emotional process mediated by power relations. A purely cognitive contribution, while relevant, is only partial.

The challenge for social researchers looking to play an active role as agents for change in the agora does not only relate to having this role recognised by others. The real challenge is to accept this role ourselves.

Case: Ezagutza Gunea, Part 1[3]

Ezagutza Gunea is an example of an agora where social researchers found a way to be part of the territorial development process – not as outsiders analysing the process, but as insiders helping to develop it.

---

3   Parts 2 and 3 of this case are presented in Chapters 2 and 3.

In 2002, EG was promoted as a network for public–private co-operation by Iraurgi Lantzen, the local development agency of Urola Erdia County (owned by the two town councils located in the county, Azpeitia and Azkoitia). It was created with the aim of improving the quality of life for inhabitants of the area by enhancing the competitiveness of local businesses. It is thus a territorial development project. Innovation and competitiveness of firms is a means to the ultimate goal, which is improved quality of life for the inhabitants.

The strategy was to focus on innovation processes and create a context in which firms could learn to develop these processes. Through the years it focused mostly on learning about how firms could improve their internal organisation (organisational innovation) and how territorial actors (town councils, firms, training centres) could improve the way they collaborated (social innovation). In the analysed period, the network was composed of the two town councils in the county, the local development agency Iraurgi Lantzen, six training centres and schools in the area, average 15 'large firms' with 50–350 employees (representing almost 90 per cent of manufacturing firms of this size in the area) and average 12 'small firms' with 10–50 employees (representing 11 per cent of manufacturing firms of this size in the area). The population of the surrounding towns is around 25,000.

All territorial actors in EG are represented on the management board that makes the strategic decisions regarding the network (strategic plans, yearly plans and budget). Firms have four representatives, training centres and town councils each have two, and the local development agency has one. Although the project was fostered by the town councils and the development agency, the chair of the board is always a firm representative, to ensure that decisions are oriented towards the needs of firms. Although the management board has a critical role in the network, specific projects are developed in self-organised work groups composed of people from every type of organisation involved in EG. The board sometimes discusses proposals arising from existing work groups, and on other occasions recognises the need to create new work groups to respond to new challenges faced by the network.

EG is a network that includes organisations corresponding to the different categories of actors described in an RIS. The knowledge application subsystem is represented by firms; government and related agencies are represented by the town councils and development agency. The knowledge generation subsystem is represented on the board by the vocational training centre. Various universities and technology centres from the region participate in the process through co-operation agreements, but they are not represented on the board as they are not located in the county. Firms participating in the network do not belong to the same value chains, sectors or clusters, and do not use the same technology or the same raw materials. What links them is that they share the same territory. Many of the managers and most of the workers live in this territory.

We propose EG as a case study for Part I because it is a good example of an agora in an RIS. It does not represent an RIS. It does not include all of the components of an RIS presented as subsystems and their interactions (the upper diagram in Figure 1.3), nor the whole set of actors in an RIS (the central diagram of Figure 1.3); it is a specific agora in the context of the RIS in the Basque Country. It is a space where some actors of the RIS, including social researchers, interact in a specific policy process.

Case Discussion: Social Researchers in the Agora

PHASE ONE: CREATING AN AGORA AND GENERATING SOCIAL INNOVATION

When EG was created in 2002, there was no other formal process in the county in which policy makers, firms and training centres were collaborating. One of the authors of this book, Miren Larrea, joined EG at a very early stage. The creation of the network had been supported by the town councils and the local development agency. A consultant developed a proposal on how to start the network, and conversations were held between the development agency and seven firms in the county about participating in the project. We entered the process with the role of co-ordinating the network. Policy makers were not explicitly looking for a researcher. However, when they saw the opportunity to hire one, they felt the link with the university would be positive. Formally, there was no researcher in the project, as the formal professional category was that of staff in the local development agency.[4] However, after ten years, we see that what most influenced the process was not the formal role assigned to us, but rather the capabilities we held and the reflection and action routines we established. These were capabilities and routines linked to social research. That is why we now consider that it was an agora.

---

4   The staff in EG are people recruited to facilitate the networking process – support actors (representatives of the different organisations in the network) to develop the collaboration processes.

Communicating the details of the project to the actors invited to participate (firms and training centres) was the core activity during the initial stage. The work method in the network was not easy to convey. Using dialogue and mutual learning as an engine for territorial development was something new. The project had to be presented in a way that would be understood by politicians, firm managers and personnel at training centres. Trust was critical, as the new process did not fit with anyone's previous frameworks of what their activity entailed. Social research was important in order to bring content to the communication process. Some elements were taken from literature on industrial districts and endogenous development. In reviewing the meeting notes and yearly plans from the first year, we can see that the concrete action plan was a mixture of demands from specific firms for training with discussion on external economies (advantages of being located in a specific place) taken from the industrial district literature, such as Becattini (1979). In a subtle way, the negotiation between societal and scientific problems that would be accepted as a solution was starting to develop in the agora.

In its first few years, the network engaged mainly in training activities (specific courses, training infrastructure and materials). However, from a territorial development point of view, there was a discussion on whether training was enough to meet the goals of the network. It was decided that it would not be enough. Another concept emerged that was more in the core of territorial development, namely the concept of knowledge management (interpreted as processes that would guarantee the development of new knowledge, not exclusively from theory, but also from the actors' own experiences). Self-managed groups for learning processes were created by firm representatives and met regularly to define what they needed to learn in order to foster change in their organisations. They invited experts in organisational fields to talk to them, but combined expert knowledge with the experience of every participant. These learning processes were included in yearly plans. The first group was formed by human resource managers, the second comprised general managers, the third production managers, the fourth team leaders, the fifth small firm managers, and the sixth R&D managers. It was a long process, as the first group was created in 2003 and the last in 2012. At the time of writing, people from 25 firms have learned to work together to support organisational innovation with the final aim of creating territorial development. The main feature was the way they related to each other and interacted in deciding on their own learning process. They were developing a new mode of interaction among firms in the county, and this was closely related to the territorial development approach that policy makers were trying to construct. Without being aware of it, they were at the core of social innovation in the county.

From a very early stage, EG was the focus of case studies written by different research teams (see Chapter 4), and the concepts proposed by the researchers were discussed by the management board. This ensured continuous open discussion about what EG was and should be.

PHASE TWO: CONNECTING SOCIAL INNOVATION WITH TECHNOLOGICAL INNOVATION

Although the process was evaluated positively by the participants, something appeared to be missing. From the start, it seemed like the project should be able to connect the learning processes to specific innovations. And when participants in the network talked about innovation, they mostly had technological innovation in mind. The situation was highlighted in a strategic reflection process in 2005, when the main challenge of advancing from knowledge management to innovation was agreed. There were contradictory feelings and reflections on this. When asked about how EG should address the issue of innovation, one of the firm representatives said: 'EG itself is the innovation.' However, it seemed that unless there were results in terms of technological innovation, the projects would not succeed.

In 2006, the network staff grew, and in 2007 a substitution was made in the co-ordination role. We (Miren Larrea) moved out of EG to a research institute, Orkestra, which will provide the case study for Part II of the book. A sociologist now stepped into the role. Up to that time, all of the network's staff had been trained in social sciences (economy, sociology and humanities). An agreement was signed between EG and Orkestra that facilitated our participation in reflection processes and projects in the network. This enabled EG to continue being an agora – a place where research and practice converged.[5]

By 2008, there was a clear feeling among the participating organisations that the county needed something to complement what was being done in EG in terms of reinforcement of technological innovation. There was an initial attempt to create a new area in EG that would support technological

---

5   An agreement was also signed with Mondragon University. Some years later, when EG was
    integrated in the Loiola Foundation, a work group was created with PhD students from the
    county who were working in different universities and technology centres in the Basque RIS.

innovation. The process started in a participatory way, following the work method used in EG. However, the agenda of politicians and the work method of the network did not fit well together. Politicians needed to have results in the short term, and the dialogue process was taking time. Consequently, politicians took the initiative outside EG. The Loiola Foundation was created in 2010 to foster technological innovation in the county; the person in charge was a telecommunications engineer. Immediately after its launch, firms and members of town councils felt the need to co-ordinate activity with EG, and the two were functionally merged into one organisation by 2011. Within one year, the new foundation had achieved results on technological innovation.[6]

During the discussion processes on co-ordinating both projects, the complementarities became clear. EG had earned recognition as a project that had managed to define a new mode of governance. In a PhD thesis developed to analyse analogous networks in the Basque Country, EG was considered one of the most advanced in terms of social innovation (Estensoro, 2012). Nevertheless, social innovation in terms of an innovative mode of governance was not enough to address the challenges faced by the county. Results were expected in terms of technological innovation. Meanwhile, it is impossible to know how the Loiola Foundation would have impacted on territorial development without the support of EG. All we can say is that the foundation's director recognised that 'the legwork done by EG paved the way for the Loiola Foundation to carry out its activities'. This complementarity was reflected in the presentations by the staff of both organisations (see Table 1.1).

Table 1.1   Definition of features of EG and the Loiola Foundation

	Ezagutza Gunea	Loiola Foundation
Orientation	Bottom-up, oriented towards responding to the needs previously identified in the network	Top-down, oriented towards bringing knowledge, innovation and technological development to the county
Goals	Seeking transformation for the development of the county	Seeking technological innovation for the development of the county
Approach to social capital (defined as trust relationships)	Creating a shared vision of the county among the involved actors: developing social capital for public–private co-operation	Enhancing the social capital generated to nurture strategic projects in the county

Source: Adapted from a presentation used by EG and the Loiola Foundation to present their functional merger.

---

6   This process is analysed in depth as the case study in Chapter 2.

While Table 1.1 was being drawn up to support the merger, dialogue was going on between us (the social researchers) and the staff of both organisations. In this dialogue the concepts of technological innovation and social innovation were discussed. The agora was again a space in which societal and scientific problems were framed and defined and where what would be accepted as a 'solution' was negotiated. We built a shared discourse that EG represented social innovation in the county and the Loiola Foundation represented technological innovation. This facilitated reflection on the complementary features of both types of innovation. The dialogue between social researchers and practitioners in the agora led to a new way of understanding territorial development on the part of the staff of both organisations and the researchers. This new understanding helped the merger process, and consequently social innovation in the county. It is an example of how the dialogue between social researchers and territorial actors fostered social innovation that facilitated technological innovation.

After the discussion of this case and reflecting on our own experience, one of the main conclusions is that one of the critical contributions social researchers can make to fostering technological innovation is social innovation – stimulating the social process to find new patterns of interaction but this was not enough in EG. The actors in the case required capabilities for both types of innovation, technological and social (see also Estensoro, 2012). The capabilities of the staff and researchers at EG were mostly related to social sciences. They created a process that produced results in terms of social innovation, but not in terms of technological innovation. When they were complemented with the capabilities of the director of the Loiola Foundation, who had capabilities for technological innovation, the results were felt to be more balanced. The capabilities for developing each type of innovation were different, and all were necessary for territorial development.

Closing Comments

When writing inside out, the case study is not a way to show the theoretical approach in practice; in fact, it is the other way around. It was the cases and our experiences in them that inspired our proposal of the agora as a space for social innovation. But what did we learn from this case about interactions in the agora that could help understand interactions in the RIS?

The first reflection on the case is that in order to foster territorial development, both types of innovation – technological and social – were necessary. Social innovation continuously reshaped how actors in the territory related to one another to learn, make decisions and take them into action. This innovation materialised among organisations in the territory as new ways of learning and co-operating with one another. The development of EG, the creation of the Loiola Foundation and their interactions were the result of social innovation in the county. None the less, in order to foster territorial development they needed to be complemented by technological innovation in new products and processes.

Figure 1.4 represents this perspective, in which territorial development depends on both social innovation and technological innovation. However, they cannot be understood as parallel processes as they shape each other, and it is in the interaction between both that territorial development takes place. Agoras are the spaces where the actors in the territory, including researchers, meet to shape both types of innovation.

We began this chapter by emphasising interaction as a key for innovation and a challenge for RISs. We return to this reflection on interactions in RISs to close this chapter. We argue that understanding social innovation can bring insight to the question posed previously around 'how' interactions can be constructed. Interaction is a social process, and defined in the terms we used, social innovation can be interpreted as innovation in interactions.

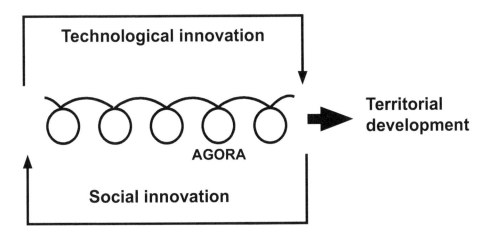

Figure 1.4   The agora, a space for social and technological innovation

If we look at an RIS from the outside, it is difficult to realise that for each actor taking part in a change, it is a unique process. Researchers that observe from the outside and just take a snapshot of a process can hardly be aware of all the meetings, all the hours of discussion, the conflicts and the fun being had, or the emotions involved with the meetings. When we do this, we are abstracting away from the processes, from the uniqueness, from the real people, from all the time that has been necessary to make them realise they must change their behaviour and from the places and territory where people work and live. When presenting the case in this first chapter, we were not explicit about all this. That is why in the next chapters we go deeper into the case presented here, trying to give a deeper insight into conflicting relationships and the construction of trust to overcome such conflicts.

As we advance through the chapters of the book, we will show how, looking from the inside out, what we see are researchers and practitioners made of flesh and blood and feelings. In the concrete meeting in the agora, the difference between researchers and practitioners is an abstraction; we all need to connect, start talking and getting to know each other if we want to create new knowledge and initiate change.

By considering all these things in the agora, we want to focus attention on issues that are not always at the core of the RIS analysis, but are necessary for understanding interaction in RISs. What do these actors have dialogue about? How do they make decisions together? How do they learn together? What are the mechanisms for moving such decisions into action?

Before we continue seeking the answers to these questions, we argue that social researchers can play a role. It is not only by analysing the process from the outside, but also by entering the dialogue with the actors and bringing a different type of knowledge. Social researchers can help accelerate the learning processes because the agora is not a static space. This means that the rules of the game used by the actors to relate to each other, the way they learn together and make decisions and the way they turn decisions into action are all continuously changing. The agora needs to be continuously reinvented, and it is in this reinvention process that social innovation and social researchers have important contributions to make. Social innovation is more than trying to make connections between people. Even when we meet someone, it will not necessarily result in anything. That is why we will explore topics such as conflict, social capital, knowledge creation and dialogue throughout the subsequent chapters. So keep reading if you want to share our path through the RIS inside out.

2

From Conflict to Consensus in the Agora

In February 2008, a mayor, one of his councillors, staff from Ezagutza Gunea and a researcher met to discuss how to improve the role local innovation policy was playing in supporting firms in the area. There was agreement on what should be done: a new organisation to support technological innovation was needed. There was a lot of energy in the meeting, and all elements seemed to be favourable for implementing this idea. Some time later, as a result of this process, a much larger meeting was held with many of the critical actors in the county. It was the opening celebration of a new foundation to support technological innovation in the area. This would have seemed easy were it not for the fact that three years and five months had passed between the first and second meetings. The mayor was no longer on the town council, and very few people at the second meeting knew about the initial reflections that had launched the process. This process was the decision to create the Loiola Foundation, which was presented in Chapter 1, as an organisation to foster technological innovation in Urola Erdia County.

In this chapter we will argue in terms of conflict and consensus in order to understand why processes in territorial development take time, even when there seems to be a clear solution to a problem. Little has been said about conflict in the RIS literature. There seems to be an assumption that conflict is bad and consensus is good. From the perspective of innovation, this is paradoxical. Schumpeter (1968) was explicit that new combinations (innovations) were a result of a creative destruction process, where the old combinations lost the competition. We believe that conflict is as natural as consensus, and that both elements are necessary in order to create the conditions for social innovation. We will continue the construction of the agora concept by describing it as the place where conflict and consensus are played out in the territory.

From a social researcher's perspective, situations like the one described above mean that when they enter an agora for territorial development with the aim of being part of the change process, the research process cannot be designed and controlled by the researcher. This breaks completely with the concept of research projects with planned processes and finishing dates, where different stages are designed at the beginning and the goal is to complete the agreed deliverables before set deadlines. Proposals look easy to implement on paper, agreements on the big missions and visions of organisations seem easy to achieve. But it is difficult to make things happen. Territory is complex. Actors as organisations have interests, priorities and pressures. Individuals representing organisations have fears, dreams, insecurities, personal agendas and aims. It is difficult to see this when the discussion relates to concepts or the big aims of territorial development such as the quality of life of inhabitants in a territory. It is easy to agree that innovation must be fostered to support competitiveness in a territory. It takes action to see that things are not so simple. It takes action to make interests, priorities, pressures, fears, insecurities and personal agendas emerge. And it is a long process to find the way to the successful implementation of action.

Conflict changes our perspective on the rhythm of territorial development and its relationship with research. Territorial development requires the agreement of actors on the type of development they want, but it requires an agreement on action in real time, not on paper. The researchers must integrate this into their agendas. It may be that research has deadlines that consensus and action cannot meet. It is important for social researchers who get involved in these kinds of processes to have the ability to adapt to the rhythm of change. But it can also transpire that action cannot wait for consensus, or even that consensus is slowed down in the short term by research because of the time required for the reflection process. This will depend on the complexity of the situation, on the extent to which conflict emerges, and on how consensus for action can be reached.

In this chapter we will first present the concept of territorial complexity, and then discuss what we mean by conflict and consensus. After that, we will again use the case of EG and the Loiola Foundation, focusing on the process of evolving from conflict to consensus on the creation of Loiola as a foundation for fostering technological innovation in the area. In the closing comments we will return to the role of researchers in handling conflict in territorial development.

Territorial Complexity

There is a situation of territorial complexity if the following three conditions are present (Karlsen, 2010). First, there must be interdependency between actors (policy makers, firms, public actors, research organisations) in a territory. There is interdependency when one actor is dependent on resources controlled by other actors and there are benefits to pooling resources (Powell, 1990).

Second, the situation is characterised by uncertainty. Uncertainty is not necessarily related to lack of information, but to the complexity of the problem itself (Koppenjan and Klijn, 2004). This is manifest in the fact that that the actors involved may disagree not only about the solution to the problem, but also about the interpretation of the problem itself. Based on the assumptions they use in the analysis, they may reach different conclusions. Scientific research no longer provides unequivocal and authoritative solutions for dealing with situations of uncertainty (Gibbons et al., 1994; Koppenjan and Klijn, 2004; Nowotny et al., 2001). This implies that traditional methods for dealing with problems in terms of intellectual design where research and research-based knowledge can be used to find the right answer no longer suffice (Koppenjan and Klijn, 2004). There is actually no 'right' solution that can solve the challenge.

Third, none of the actors has the power to direct others' actions in a specific direction, and no one has the necessary resources to solve the challenge alone. The two traditional approaches – market and government (hierarchy) – do not offer satisfying solutions in these situations. The market approach is based on independence between actors' preferences and choices, and the hierarchy approach is based on dependency (Powell, 1990). They offer no solutions for situations of interdependency, such as those represented in territorial complexity. In such situations, since none of the actors has the power to direct others' actions nor the necessary resources to solve the challenge alone, they have to collaborate (Karlsen, 2010). They have to collaborate in order to generate a shared interpretation of the situation, and must agree in making the necessary decisions and actions. Collaboration is a process in which actors share information, resources, responsibility, rewards and risks in order to achieve a common goal; it involves engagement and trust, and takes time, effort and dedication. It is a collective process. However, there is no guarantee that the situation will be resolved. It is only in the future that one will be able to judge whether a decision was 'correct'. In this kind of situation there are no other ways to judge the quality of a solution than to test it through final actions, and not through final arguments. The results of the actions can only be seen and judged in the long term.

Solutions thus require social innovation in the terms defined in Chapter 1. Agoras can be adequate spaces to explore such new modes of interaction and collaboration. One of the contexts where agoras for territorial development are constructed is that of policy networks. This is the type of agora we will focus on from now on in Part I.

There is a rich variety of discussions and definitions of networks and policy networks in the academic literature; for an extensive discussion on the roots of the concept of the policy network, see Klijn (1997). This concept is used within political science to analyse policy processes 'as complex interactions where many actors participate and where processes are ambiguous as a result of multiple goals and strategies of actors and of uncertainty about information and outcomes' (Kickert et al., 1997, p. 6). In policy networks there is interdependency between actors. Policy networks are a means to handle situations of territorial complexity.

In this book we define policy networks as more or less stable patterns of interactions between interdependent actors, which are organised and shaped around territorial complexity with the goal of fostering territorial development. They mostly materialise in terms of public–private partnerships, where policy is shaped by all, not just by politicians. Collaboration requires some kind of governance – steering or management. One of the critical elements for understanding the development of these policy networks is shared leadership, defined not as formal authority, but as the capacity to influence peers in a collective process where interdependent actors have to collaborate in order to attain an objective (Karlsen and Larrea, 2012; Pearce and Conger, 2003). A policy network is an agora when there are researchers *participating* in the process, not just observing it from the outside. Such participation and the mutual influence of the rest of the actors on researchers and researchers on the rest of actors implies that researchers participate in the shared leadership of the process.

Conflict and Consensus

Our approach to handling territorial complexity departs from the concepts of conflict and consensus. Conflict is a situation where different actors have different values, experiences, interests, resources and approaches to a given situation. It can vary in intensity from low to high disagreement, and it can also vary in scope, from few to many actors involved (Karlsen, 2010; Koppenjan, 2007). Consensus is a situation where there is enough agreement among actors to make action possible. We have adopted the term 'consensus' as part of the conflict–consensus dichotomy instead of using 'agreement' because there may be different levels of agreement, but the situation is qualitatively different whether such agreement is or is not enough for action to take place. This does not mean that they agree in everything or that everybody agrees. It means that there is enough agreement that a change process can be initiated or proceed. It means that the actors that disagree respect the solution to act.

When conflict has been discussed in RISs, it has often been discussed in terms of conflict between the subsystems, which would imply a non-functioning innovation system. But this is an abstract discussion. By integrating the concept of agora into RISs, we propose to understand conflict and consensus not in terms of subsystems, but in terms of concrete networks of actors in RISs (see Figure 1.3 in Chapter 1). This helps researchers to approach conflict in a more concrete way, as the position of actors in the network defines power play and confronted interests. Besides, although we have said that when we talk about territorial actors we are referring to organisations, the gap between organisations and the persons who represent them can be another source of conflict. Individuals are not always completely aligned with the views, goals and interests of the organisation they represent. Or, as we said in the introduction to the book when we defined actors, they may simply lack all the information to represent the whole of their organisation.

It is very difficult for a researcher to develop a good insight into the interests, power plays, hidden agendas, distrust and so on that are affecting the process. But this is critical knowledge in facing their most challenging task, which is to contribute to solving the situation through research – to lead the actors from a situation of conflict to consensus. This must be handled in a way that uses the energy from a conflict in a positive mode to create common ground for taking the necessary actions on the path to reaching consensus.

This difficulty is strengthened by the fact that conflict and consensus must be understood as pluralistic and multi-level. A complex set of diverse actors is needed to solve conflict and create consensus to act, and such actors sometimes have influence at a very local level, such as municipality or county level, sometimes at a regional level, and sometimes at national or international level.

It is difficult to solve territorial complexity without understanding the role each of them plays and how they affect others.

The participation of social researchers in agoras is a way to advance understanding of the complexity of conflict and consensus in RISs. Conflict and consensus form a cyclical continuum where a situation can change from conflict to consensus and from consensus to conflict through different actions over time. The path to resolving conflict requires connecting to each other and sharing differences through dialogue. The role of the agora is to generate the necessary time and space for connection and dialogue to take place. Dialogue to solve conflict and reach consensus for action is thus an important part of territorial development. This same dialogue is a critical element to enable social researchers to understand how conflict can be handled in RISs. The concept of dialogue in the agora will be developed further in Part III. One of the critical points in fostering territorial development in agoras is understanding that conflicting stages in territorial complexity are natural, and must not be avoided, hidden under the carpet or ignored. In order to handle conflict and consensus, it is important to avoid a simplistic view of conflict as a bad thing and consensus as a good thing.

Conflict can be good as long as it implies that new insight, knowledge and innovations are created in the process. Conflict can break lock-in situations and create new development paths, while consensus can create a situation of lock-in. Of course, unresolved conflict between actors can damage the functioning of an RIS. But in the long run consensus can reduce the innovative capacity of the innovation system. Agoras can play a role in the development of a constructive approach to conflict in a territory, and social research can make a significant contribution to this approach.

Analytical Frameworks on Conflict and Consensus

There are no recipes for researchers who want to be part of the process of handling conflict to reach consensus. But the conflict–consensus dimension can be used as an analytical tool in order to understand situations of territorial complexity and try to solve them. We will now share two such analytical frameworks, which have been useful for us in various territorial development processes when the time has come to discuss situations perceived as conflict. An analytical framework for analysing territorial complexity is presented in Figure 2.1. There are two dimensions in the framework: aims of the actors (for example territorial development, innovation, increased competitiveness and increased quality of life) and means (for example economic tools, organisation of territorial development work, and roles and responsibilities of different actors). Figure 2.1 illustrates that in any territorial challenge it is possible to find either conflict or consensus among the actors affected. Making it very simple, there are consequently four possible situations for every territorial challenge.

The dichotomy between aims and means becomes artificial in real-life situations. Consensus about aims often appears easy to achieve. In many policy processes, networks or strategic reflections actors easily agree on large and abstract aims such as improving the innovation and competitiveness of firms or improving the quality of life of citizens. This kind of consensus is easy on paper. But as steps are taken towards the concrete definition of means and actions, contradictions start to emerge in the deep understanding of what such grand aims mean for territorial actors. A shared understanding of the meaning and implications of concepts such as territorial development, competitiveness and innovation needs to be constructed with the participation of the interdependent actors in the RIS. It is in this process of construction of shared meanings that agoras are needed, and social researchers can play a role.

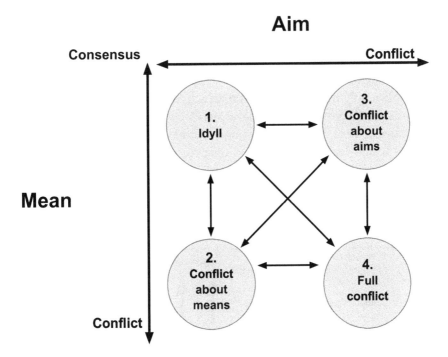

Figure 2.1   Different types of territorial complexity
Source: Karlsen (2010), p. 97.

The framework can be used to discuss the cyclical perspective of conflict and consensus. Its use can help a group to develop awareness that the construction of consensus for action is not the result of a specific agreement at a determined moment in time. It is the result of a dialogue that develops among territorial actors in the long run, where the balance between conflict and consensus continuously changes. When the process reaches a point of consensus, there is a window of opportunity to act, which might change the balance again. With a new balance, new conflicts may emerge, which will generate the need to continue with the dialogue and try to reach a new consensus at another point in time.

In order to understand how the transition from conflict to consensus happens we have been using another framework, presented in Table 2.1. In this case it is essential to be clear that both conflict and consensus can be implicit or explicit, because neither conflict nor consensus are always expressed explicitly (Karlsen and Larrea, 2012). It is necessary to make conflict explicit in order to handle it and to construct consensus. Many networks for territorial development stagnate because participants do not feel that the network is relevant enough to face the costs of making conflict explicit.

We have said that the agora is naturally a space in conflict. But what we add now is that most of the conflict remains implicit in the agora. The goal is not to make all conflict explicit; this would be a way to stop development. The process is to detect conflicts that are hindering development, because these are the ones that might make the process stagnate. Once detected, such conflicts must be made explicit only if (or to the extent to which) they can be managed and led to some process of construction of consensus. A conflict made explicit without a constructive process can destroy dialogue, and a conflict made explicit and not handled can also lead to stagnation of the process.

Table 2.1   Different situations of consensus and conflict

	Consensus	Conflict
Explicit	1. Explicit consensus: 'We agree, and let it be known in the network.'	3. Explicit conflict: 'We let the others know we disagree.'
Implicit	2. Implicit consensus: 'We tacitly agree, but do not take any action to share the agreement.'	4. Implicit conflict: 'We tacitly disagree, but we do not take any action to make the disagreement known.'

Source: Karlsen and Larrea (2012), p. 222.

Case: Ezagutza Gunea, Part 2

In Chapter 1 we introduced Ezagutza Gunea as an agora. We also briefly introduced the Loiola Foundation and its creation process. We return to that aspect of the case by focusing on the process which occurred between the points when need for a new structure for technological innovation was made explicit in EG (in February 2008), when Loiola began operating (September 2010), and when EG integrated operatively with Loiola (April 2011).

As stated previously, in February 2008 EG had been successful in generating social innovation, but not technological innovation. This was felt as a pressure. A committee was established within EG consisting of staff from EG, two politicians and a social researcher (Miren Larrea). The aim was to explore how EG could be used as a tool for innovation policy at the local level. At that time we had not approached the concept of social innovation, and when we said 'innovation', we meant technological innovation. In October 2008 the committee made a formal proposal to the management board of EG which contained two new elements. The first was the creation of a work group within EG involving firms' R&D and innovation managers. The second was the creation of a new organisation linked to EG and directly oriented towards entrepreneurship and technological innovation which would adopt a more hierarchical approach than the rest of EG (not every project would need to be a co-operation project, as in EG). Figure 2.2 illustrates the proposal for both changes. We are aware that it is not easy for the reader to interpret this diagram. However, we have decided to include it in order to later reflect on what it takes to make an idea like this move from paper to becoming actionable.

The management board of EG accepted the proposal from the committee, and the dialogue process with the rest of the network members began. The process was evolving following the participatory decision making method in EG, and staff discussed the proposal with firms and training centres. But politicians were under pressure from political agendas and needed to get tangible results within a shorter period. They took the process out of the participatory framework of EG and channelled it through the local development agency, which had a more hierarchical structure, and thus the ability to create a foundation more rapidly than EG.

In terms of conflict and consensus, we argue that although there was apparent consensus about the aims, conflict emerged about the means.

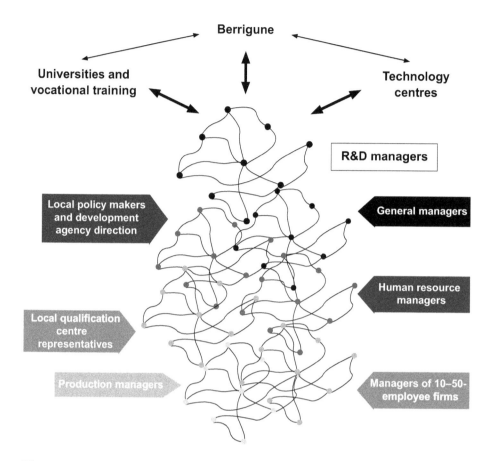

Figure 2.2   Berrigune, an agreement on paper to foster technological
                innovation

The participatory process and dialogue in the agora stopped. Thus, conflict was not made explicit and resolved, but simply avoided. At that time, the decision making mode of the network was considered too slow to take the project into action, so action was undertaken outside the network. As a consequence, Loiola was created as a foundation independent of EG.

After the Loiola Foundation was created, the question of how the new organisation related to EG remained. Many firms, the town councils and the agency were participating in both organisations. In 2010, the firms and town councils claimed that it was not rational for a county as small as Urola Erdia to have two organisations, and that they should be merged to one. A new process began, led by a committee with participants from both organisations (mostly the firms), with the aim of connecting these two organisations.

As researchers linked into EG through a collaboration agreement, we were invited to reflect on the process by the staff of both organisations. We assisted reflection using concepts such as governance, or top-down and bottom-up approaches to territorial development. We were contributing to the dialogue process that would move the situation from conflict to consensus. The new organisation that functionally fused the two previous organisations is illustrated in Figure 2.3.

This new structure was presented and discussed, first with the board and later with individual members of EG. After this round, the new organisational structure was finally approved by the management board, following a process lasting a few months. Altogether, it had taken more than three years to evolve from conflict to consensus for action. We will now discuss our main lessons from the process.

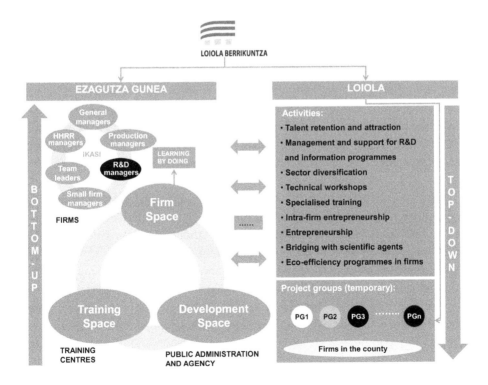

Figure 2.3   The merged organisation of Ezagutza Gunea and the Loiola Foundation

Case Discussion: Managing Conflict in the Long Term

There are many elements in Figure 2.2 that can also be found in Figure 2.3, though it is drawn in a different way. The main differences are not in the concepts, but in the meaning they held for the participants. The main difference is that Figure 2.2 represents only consensus on paper, while Figure 2.3 represents consensus taken to action, which took more than three years. There is a large gap between solutions on paper and actionable solutions. In the following sections we will divide the process that took place between the discussions of Figure 2.2 and the implementation of Figure 2.3 into five steps to discuss some critical elements.

GENERATING AWARENESS OF CONFLICT IN THE AGORA

We believe that the situation described above is not unusual. We actually think it is quite common for there to be conflicts between actors in a territory. But as we said earlier, it is difficult to find much in the RIS literature about conflict, how it can be resolved and how research can contribute to the construction of consensus. The interpretation of public–private partnership often avoids the relevance of conflict and only tells success stories about consensus. These biased stories can influence territorial development processes if actors try to avoid conflict instead of addressing it directly. Situations where there is apparent consensus or consensus only on the major aims but where nothing concrete happens are often situations where there is implicit conflict. This can bring stagnation to an organisation and territory. We believe, as we said, that one of the roles of social researchers in territorial development is to help actors to make conflict explicit in a constructive way. The concepts and frameworks social researchers bring can facilitate these kinds of processes.

Even if conflict is natural, there are few researchers in the academic community related to territorial development who see involvement in conflict as a natural part of their role. Actually, it is not that easy to see concrete conflict when we interpret RISs in terms of subsystems. Nevertheless, firms compete among themselves in markets and in the labour market. Policy makers from different government levels, even different departments in the same level of government, have conflicting perspectives on issues related to development. The complexity increases when different political parties have to interact. Universities compete with each other for students and funds. The same applies to vocational training centres. There are also conflicting approaches among technology centres, mainly due to the scarcity of funds. Conflict can also appear when actors from different subsystems meet in a process.

The understanding of a territorial development process, its priorities, agenda and rhythm, are perceived differently by firms than by politicians or universities and other knowledge organisations. The policy process is highly influenced by elections. Projects from one administration are questioned by the next. Trust relationships in policy networks are very much influenced by a change of political leaders. Policy makers have an urge to communicate results in the media. Firms often perceive that processes proceed too slowly at universities and technology centres. As researchers, we often disagree with this perspective, but we realise that our models on paper hardly take the step to action. All these are the ordinary features of an agora for territorial development, and they are more than anecdotal – they are the core of the agora.

MAKING CONFLICT EXPLICIT: THE NEED FOR RULES

There are no recipes for constructing agoras that will help to handle conflict. But it is important to design agoras in anticipation that different actors will have different perspectives and interests. Rules and routines must be defined from the beginning so that they facilitate the process of making conflict explicit and work with it to construct consensus. Simple issues like who can call meetings, who decides the agenda, how decisions will be made if there is no agreement or who will implement the decisions made need to be decided. But these rules and routines are often based on the good will of the participants and have no legal status. The story of EG can help us to see how rules were defined to help handle conflict. These are seen most clearly in the management board of EG.

In Chapter 1 we introduced the management board of EG as composed of representatives of all kinds of actors participating in the network (two representatives of the town councils, one from the agency, four from firms, and two from training centres). The president of the board is always a representative of a firm. So although town councils assume a critical part of the financing and launched the project, decisions about the strategy of the network and annual plans and budgets are made by a board where policy makers (elected politicians and the director of the development agency) have three votes out of nine. In this context, territorial complexity is clear, as the actors on the board are interdependent, but none has the formal authority to direct others' actions, and they need to co-operate. Besides, the balance between the votes represents the need to reach agreement, as none of the types of actors representing any of the subsystems of the RIS have enough votes to force a decision on their own.

But this design and these rules for collaboration were not enough in February 2008. An initial dialogue about the new organisation had begun in EG, but when conflict emerged, the project's established rules were abandoned by policy makers. In a situation of territorial complexity, none of the actors can force others to follow the rules. It is only the shared learning process that can make a difference. It is through such a process that the participants come to believe that the collectively constructed outcome is more beneficial for each of the parts than one constructed individually. In 2008 and 2011, the rules were the same on paper. But in 2011, critical actors shared a common perspective on the benefits of the participatory process. The conclusion is quite simple to state and very difficult to do. The goal is not to have rules on paper that will foster dialogue among the participants. The goal is to have a learning process that will shape the attitudes and behaviour of the participants in the agora and encourage them to stick to such rules even when decisions are difficult.

Many management boards, committees and administration boards of public–private partnerships for territorial development work with a philosophy developed for hierarchical structures. They seldom meet, are disconnected from the day-to-day development of the project, analyse the proposals and make the overall decisions. They do not go deep enough into the project to develop a shared vision. Deep inside, some hardly believe the partnership will bring better results for their organisations than they can achieve on their own. Often they are part of the process because it is politically useful, because they have been invited by someone they want to be on good terms with. Such spaces are agoras on paper. Social researchers can play a role in these contexts, helping participants to develop new perspectives on the process by discussing different concepts and frameworks related to their situation and possible solutions. The challenge for the social researcher, together with the rest of participants, is thus to transform agoras on paper into agoras that shape behaviour. In the case of Figure 2.2, the diagram itself was drawn by a researcher and proposed for discussion with actors. In Figure 2.3, the researcher participated in the prior discussions and the diagram was constructed by the staff of EG and the Loiola Foundation. In both cases, the social researcher was one more actor in the dialogue who contributed from a specific angle – the perspective of social research.

FACING CONFLICT BETWEEN NETWORK AND HIERARCHY

Many of the agoras defined as public–private partnerships among actors from the different subsystems of the RIS are fostered by public policy, more specifically by innovation and competitiveness policies. They are policy networks in the terms defined earlier in this chapter. They aim to incorporate private firms and other actors in the knowledge subsystem into the policy process. The main argument for them is that everybody's knowledge is necessary to define the right processes and programmes and to create territorial environments that support innovation by firms. The case of EG and the Loiola Foundation follows this pattern.

There is a type of conflict that most policy networks face in their development path. We could call it the *foundational conflict*, as it is a conflict about how other conflicts will be handled. It is often related to the fact that policy makers are accustomed to making decisions in hierarchical structures. Public–private partnership requires a type of dialogue that differs from the hierarchies of each organisation and sits actors in front of each other on equal terms, though with different roles. The learning process to resolve this conflict between networks and hierarchies will determine the sustainability of the partnership. There is no global solution for the conflict between networks and hierarchy in the RIS. From the perspective shared in Figure 1.3 in Chapter 1, where we positioned agoras in the RIS, every policy network or agora will have to go through their own specific awareness and learning processes to overcome this conflict.

When the mayor first agreed to foster the creation of a new organisation for technological innovation in 2008, he agreed that it should be part of the evolving network of EG. The staff defined a participatory process for determining what such an organisation should be. Dialogue had begun, but it was taking time. The process could not respond to the political agenda, and politicians needed a quicker response. They made the decision to take the project out of the network and its rules for decision making, and moved it into the local development agency, where the elected policy makers had the hierarchical position to make faster decisions than within the network. A new foundation was then established relatively quickly. But conflict had not been solved; from the first meeting, the need to integrate EG and the new organisation made it evident that this was so.

Network governance based on participatory processes can be a double-edged sword. Evolving from conflict to consensus takes time and dialogue. There is no short cut to constructing consensus. It might be tempting to jump to action quickly, and hierarchy can be faster than networks. But if consensus has not been constructed in the process, projects will be jeopardised. When a participatory process is abandoned halfway, it will create the feeling that these processes are not useful. There is often a temptation to abandon them and go back to hierarchical structures to make faster decisions. Our argument is that although they might seem easier to start with, hierarchical decisions have limited capabilities to resolve territorial complexity.

KEEPING THE DIALOGUE GOING

In order to avoid hierarchy taking over the networking process, the facilitators of the process must have the capabilities to make it resilient. In Chapter 1 we said that the staff of EG were hired as facilitators of the networking process. EG and its management board had been carefully designed as agoras for dialogue, but the moment came when some of the actors took a specific issue out of this agora. However, the issue at stake was critical for the EG members. The process of building consensus out of conflict might have stopped there, but the staff of EG continued informal dialogue with politicians and firms, and as soon as the director of the new organisation was appointed, with her. At that moment, the agora moved from the formal spaces designed for it into informal spaces. Agoras are where the real dialogue is developing, and this is not always in the spaces formally designed for it. Dialogue must not stop, and the role of the facilitators is to keep dialogue going continuously. The contribution of social research in these contexts is to create new opportunities for dialogue by presenting concepts and frameworks that can help facilitators make the dialogue evolve in new directions – directions that can avoid stagnation.

Formal spaces are important, and designing them adequately to enable dialogue is critical. But, as we said earlier, in a long-term process there will be times when the dialogue takes place in the formal agora, and times when it develops in the informal one. In EG, dialogue was restored in the formal agora as soon as possible, but this took time. It took a collective definition and acceptance of the rules, which was developed mainly in the informal space and was led by the staff (facilitators) of EG and the Loiola Foundation.

One of the challenges for social researchers in these processes is being able to participate in the informal processes. How can we justify continued dialogue with actors during the periods when there is no specific research project in place? In this case it was possible because the link to the process was not a specific project or programme, but the long-term involvement of the social researcher with the facilitators of a process in the context of a very flexible collaboration agreement. Researchers and practitioners had learnt to share reflection processes throughout the years, and the end of the formal projects did not lead to the end of this dialogue. The discussions of concepts such as top-down and bottom-up approaches to development, new governance modes, open innovation, territorial innovation systems and the complementarities between social, technological and organisational innovation were discussed informally, outside any formal research project. However, they still influenced the proposal presented in Figure 2.3. This engagement of researchers in change processes, which is difficult to achieve in the organisational structures of most research organisations, is an issue we will address in Part II.

MAKING TERRITORIAL DEVELOPMENT POSSIBLE

We have described the process of dialogue in EG as a learning process that took from 2008 to 2011. We will now try to understand what really changed through dialogue in the agora to help it reach an actionable consensus in 2011.

The dialogue for consensus in EG cannot be simplified into a specific moment and place where all actors met. It was a process of a different nature. We could call it *diffuse dialogue*. There was a multiplicity of group meetings where different actors interacted among themselves, focusing mainly on issues of organisational innovation and county development, individual meetings with staff where actors openly expressed themselves, and meetings of the board where each participant represented a stakeholder group. This diffuse approach reveals the critical role of the network's staff as facilitators of the process. They were the ones who were present throughout all meetings and formal conversations. They were the ones who could most easily detect conflict arising, the ones who could best facilitate the elements of consensus and generate the moments when such consensus could emerge and be shared. This was actually one of their main roles, together with facilitating learning processes.

But what had changed between 2008, when the process was taken from the network to the hierarchy, and 2011? First, in 2011 there were better contextual conditions for making conflict explicit. In 2008 it was felt that there was a need to create an organisation that would support technological innovation, but the general economic context was positive, nobody was yet investing money in such a project, and it was mainly politicians who had publicly declared the need for such an organisation. In 2011 the situation of crisis in the whole region and country was evident, and the feeling that technological innovation was part of the answer was clear – the foundation had already been created, and firms and town councils had invested in it. They felt they had more to lose if a solution was not found.

Second, conflict had had time to mature and contradictions were clearer, so it was easier for town councils and firms to make them explicit. It was at this moment when conflict was made explicit that the staff of both organisations could take the dialogue back to the formal agoras of EG and the Loiola Foundation and deliver a proposal for co-ordination. Both situations, in 2008 and 2011, were situations of territorial complexity. But in between, a shared learning process had taken place. The mayor who had made the decision to create Loiola as a foundation independent from EG played a critical role in unifying the two projects. In a meeting with him and other policy makers, we agreed that one of the main lessons we all had learnt was that networks might take longer to launch a process at the beginning, because constructing the initial consensus takes time. But once the process has been launched, it is this consensus that gives speed to the implementation.

Figure 2.3 might not be a researcher's ideal design when departing exclusively from literature on RISs, public–private partnerships and territorial development, but it had the potential to fit the expectations of all participating actors. That led to a much higher probability of implementation than a theoretically sharper design. The role of research was not to contribute a whole proposed solution. It was to provide the participants, and most directly the facilitators of the process, with concepts and frameworks that were helpful at every stage of the process. Some of the concepts and frameworks were just ignored, others rejected, and others used as building blocks to construct their own solutions. These solutions might seem imperfect from an exclusively theoretical point of view, but they were the result of a collective construction of a solution, which meant that conflicting perspectives were being integrated into shaping the best actionable solution. Researchers were aware that theory would have brought to the table a solution that looked better on paper, but this would not have been actionable as it would not have integrated the conflicting perspectives.

Conflict can stagnate if it is not handled, but it is also important to let it grow to the point where it is clearly perceived by participants in the process. Staff or researchers in a process must avoid making conflict explicit before the affected actors are fully aware of it and ready to assume responsibility for resolving it. But staff and researchers must actively open the dialogue channels that will make this awareness grow. It is a delicate balance, but concepts and frameworks from social research can play a critical role in helping actors reflect on and understand territorial complexity situations. Research can take the discussion from the completely concrete effects of everyday work to a more analytical level where the whole system can be better understood by participants and conflict can be discussed from a less personal perspective. This facilitates the process of making awareness of conflict grow in a constructive way.

Closing Comments

This case study enabled the discussion of how territorial development can be seen as a process of making conflict explicit in situations of territorial complexity, then managing this conflict to reach consensus and action. In this context the agora is seen as the space for dialogue between science and the public (researchers and territorial actors) that facilitates the transformation of conflict into consensus.

What the case study showed is that there can be a moment when researchers seem to have a solution on paper and communicate it to practitioners. At this moment there is often even apparent consensus on the solution. But there are also conflicting interests that make actors behave differently from what was expected following the discussion of the solution on paper.

Avoiding or ignoring conflict can generate a feeling of advancing quickly in the short term. In the medium and long term it can stagnate and hinder a development process, as implicit conflict has more influence on the behaviour of actors than explicit consensus.

Traditionally, social researchers end their role in the agora when the solution on paper is delivered. We argue that the agora, as a space for dialogue that mutually shapes researchers and practitioners, must continue making conflict explicit and working on the conflict until actual behaviour is changed and action takes place in an improved way.

In Table 2.2 we try to synthesise some of the elements of conflict avoiding and conflict facing approaches to the agora.

Table 2.2   Two different approaches to conflict in the agora

	Conflict-avoiding approach	Conflict-facing approach
Approach to change	Change is approached as new solutions on paper	Change is approached as new behaviour
Approach to conflict and consensus	Avoidance of conflict, assumption that consensus on paper leads to action	Integration of conflict as a natural element in the process, ongoing dialogue to transform consensus on paper into consensus in behaviour
Approach to agora	Agora interpreted as a space for linear knowledge transfer	Agora interpreted as a space for a mutual shaping
Role of the social researcher	Make recommendations	Enter dialogue with concepts and frameworks

We said in the discussion previously that solutions derived from managing conflict often reflect a balance between conflicting interests and do not always look as theoretically perfect as solutions on paper. For a researcher who does not integrate conflict as a relevant factor in the analysis, it may be difficult to accept the final action as 'good enough', as the comparison is made with the ideal proposal on paper. But even when the researcher is ready to accept it as 'good enough', it can be difficult to have an open discussion on conflict, either because participants lack the frameworks to make it explicit or because they expect the solution not to be worth the cost of making conflict explicit. This means that there may be aspects of conflict that actors decide to keep implicit. The researcher in the agora who wants to maintain a conflict-facing approach must create the conditions for integrating the conflicting perspectives of actors in the dialogue in the agora – even in situations where they are only made explicit in informal agoras or are made only partly explicit. Chapter 3 presents some of our reflections on how this challenge can be faced by constructing social capital and collective knowing.

3

Social Capital and Collective Knowing in the Agora

In early 2005, when EG had been operating for two and a half years, a questionnaire was completed by all participating actors (firms, town councils, training centres and the local development agency) to evaluate the network. When asked about their *motivation to enter the network*, 31 per cent answered that they had entered to avoid being left out, 38 per cent answered that they wanted to develop shared projects, and 31 per cent answered that they were conscious that they needed to co-operate to improve competitiveness. Asked about their *motivations to remain in the network*, the answers varied. Nobody answered that they remained in the network in order to avoid being left out. The majority (84 per cent) responded that they remained in order to develop shared projects, and only 16 per cent said they co-operated in order to improve competitiveness. It took two more years for the representative of one of the firms to show an even deeper change. She put it in a nutshell by saying: 'When we started I came here to see what I could get out of this for my firm. Nowadays I come because I want my children to have a future in this county.'

Territorial development in the agora is a collective process. It benefits individual actors, but it cannot be constructed on the basis of exclusively individual benefits. When a process begins, the collective perspective is often not there and actors are mainly motivated by the individual benefits for their organisations. However, as time goes by a deeper change process around building a shared vision among collaborating actors emerges. The shared vision cannot be constructed unless there is a structure (formal or informal) that makes interaction possible and the different actors trust each other. That is why we will argue for the need for social capital in territorial development and, more concretely, in agoras for territorial development.

In the previous chapter we argued that researchers must not avoid conflict when working in the agora. We will use the concept of social capital to reflect on how this can be done. But social capital is not the aim in itself, but a means to something else. The goal in the agora is to generate what we call *collective knowing*. Its definition comes from the distinction between knowledge as a stock and knowing as a process of knowledge in action. In short, the argument is that knowledge is a stock that can be changed into knowing through a development process in which social capital is needed. But as the means to a goal, social capital must adjust to the goals of each specific territorial development process, as there is no generic mode of social capital that is valid for all such processes. The role of the social researcher in the agora is not only to generate knowledge, but also to create the social capital that will support its transformation into collective knowing.

In order to reflect on these concepts we will continue using the case of EG. The discussion of this case will show that, from our point of view, the development of collective knowing and a shared vision is not a homogenising exercise that will lead everybody to think the same things. It leads to diversity as a source of development. The challenge is to generate social capital without neutralising diversity.

The contents of this chapter have been structured so that we will first present the concepts of knowledge, knowing and social capital, and based on them we will propose our approach to collective knowing and link this concept to policy learning. After that, we will describe a specific project in EG, and use this as the basis for a discussion of how social capital and knowledge influence the creation of collective knowing. The closing comments will take the discussion into the policy learning field.

Knowledge Versus Knowing

There is a difference between knowledge and knowing. In English, the word 'knowledge' is a noun, while 'knowing' is a form of the verb 'to know'. As a noun, 'knowledge' can be interpreted as a stock. As a verb, 'knowing' can be interpreted as an action or a process (Karlsen, 2007). Knowledge presupposes a fixed point in time when some insight or belief qualifies as knowledge, while knowing is what continuously unfolds as we make use of knowledge in action (Styhre, 2003). In order to introduce this debate in relation to the agora, we make a distinction between theoretical knowledge and knowing. Theoretical knowledge is what is expressed in books by academics; it is declarative knowledge. This is also labelled as 'know-that' (Ryle, 1949) or 'know-what' (Polanyi, 1966). Ryle (1949) distinguished between know-that and knowing how. The latter is the ability to do something, to use intelligence in action. Knowing how emerges through the application of knowledge in a given context. For Ryle, intelligence is more manifest in the way people act than in the way people think. He therefore argues in favour of *knowing how in action*, because theorists have been so preoccupied with the task of investigating the nature, source and credentials of the theories we adopt that they have for the most part ignored the question of what it is for someone to know how to perform a task (Ryle, 1949, p. 28).

In the academic debate, when a problem is solved in a theoretical article, the discussion moves on to the next issue at stake. But can we assume that such a problem can also be solved in reality? A theoretical argument is an abstraction from reality. It is what we have called a solution on paper. It is stock knowledge. Experience shows that there are no territorial development recipes – when a solution is stated on paper, it does not mean that we can just follow the recipe and it will be implemented. Most policy makers and researchers are aware that it is not that easy. Still, the actions of many policy makers and researchers seem to fit with that pattern. That is the reason why we distinguish between knowledge and *knowing how*. Arguing for a perspective or an action is not the same as doing the action, nor does it mean that the action can actually be done. The arguments can be purely theoretical, abstract and general in form, which means that they are not necessarily applicable in a given context.

The challenge is not to distinguish knowledge and knowing how; it is to combine different kinds of knowing how in order to innovate. To make such combinations requires people with knowing how, which is developed always in practice (Karlsen, 2007).

Polanyi (1966, p. 7) draws the conclusion that *we can know more than we can tell*. Tacit knowing is an integrated part of every action. This implies that we cannot describe explicitly and accurately every part of an action, but we can still do an action. It is simply not possible to put into words every aspect of an action. This makes tacit knowing an integral part of knowing how. Polanyi uses the example of the ability to recognise a face in a crowd of people. His observation is that we cannot 'tell' why we can recognise a face, but we can still do it. Polanyi's argument is that there is knowledge we as individuals have which is hard to express in words.

This poses some challenges for the social researcher in the agora. Territorial development depends not only on knowledge, but on knowing. And it is not possible to identify tacit knowing by interviewing people. Tacit knowing can only be identified in action by observing people in action. The researcher needs a position in the agora which is connected to action in order to relate not only to knowledge, but also to knowing. According to Polanyi, it is not possible to distinguish knowing from the action in itself – to separate knowing from the subject.

The last element in our argument is that the agora is a place for collective knowing. In the literature there is an ongoing discourse around whether there is a difference between the individual and the collective. At the one extreme is Simon (1991), who argues that all learning takes place in the individual and that organisations learn by adding new members to the organisation. Simon (1991) does not see any difference between the individual and the collective, while others, such as Berger and Luckmann (1966), Nelson and Winter (1982), Brown and Duguid (1991), Weick and Roberts (1993), Spender (1994), Nahapiet and Ghoshal (1998) and Orlikowski (2002), argue strongly that there is a difference. The main argument from these authors is that any collective unit, such as a group, an organisation or the actors in an agora, is not reducible to what a single individual knows. People working together develop and share knowledge as a collective effort and product – as collective knowing (Greenwood and Levin, 2005). Our approach to collective knowing reflects the latter approach and is closely linked to the concept of social capital.

Social Capital

Social capital is defined by Putnam (1995, pp. 664–5) as *features of social life – networks, norms and trust – that enable participants to act together more effectively to pursue shared objectives*. Interaction is a precondition for the development and maintenance of dense social capital (Bourdieu, 1986; Nahapiet and Ghoshal, 1998). It is thus a concept that gives insight into what we need to change when we talk about social innovation as innovation in the way actors interact in the agora for territorial development (see Chapter 1).

The concept of social capital has increased in popularity since the early 1990s (Wollebæk and Segaard, 2011; Fine, 2007; Fine, 2010; Farr, 2004; Farr, 2007).[1]

---

1   For an introduction to the concept, see Farr (2004; 2007), and for a critique of the concept, see Fine (2010; 2007).

Social capital makes possible the achievement of aims that could not be achieved by a single individual without extra cost (Nahapiet and Ghoshal, 1998). It is thus a resource that can be used to solve collective dilemmas, such as territorial complexity.

Social capital is one of the forms of capital that increases rather than decreases through use (Nahapiet and Ghoshal, 1998). It is owned by the members of a group, but no actor has exclusive rights on that capital. Social capital is not the answer to all questions. It can have both positive and negative effects. It can facilitate some kinds of action, and hamper others. For example, high levels of trust in social relationships reduce the need for costly monitoring, while low levels make it necessary to develop monitoring systems. High levels of trust can reduce transaction costs, while low levels can increase them. Strong norms and mutual identification can have a positive effect on behaviour in specific groups and in specific places in the territory, but at the same time can limit openness to information and hamper the creation of innovations.

In order to develop the discussion of the case, we will mainly use the approach proposed by Nahapiet and Ghoshal (1998). One of the strongest links between our approaches is that social capital is not a goal in itself, but a means. In their case, they analyse the role of social capital in the creation of intellectual capital in inter-firm relationship contexts. In our case, we talk about knowing in agoras for territorial development.

Nahapiet and Ghoshal (1998) argue that social capital has three dimensions: the structural, the relational and the cognitive. The structural dimension is the impersonal configuration of linkages between actors. This dimension is usually described in measurable terms such as numbers of linkages between actors, which can be further described in such terms as patterns of density, connectivity and hierarchy.

The relational dimension is harder to measure than the structural dimension. This dimension describes the kinds of personal relationships people have developed with each other through a history of interactions. Personal relationships take time to develop. Among the key factors in this dimension are trust and trustworthiness, norms and sanctions, obligations and expectations, and identity and identification (Nahapiet and Ghoshal, 1998).

The last dimension is the cognitive, which is referred to as shared representations, interpretations and systems of meaning among parties

(Nahapiet and Ghoshal, 1998; Cicourel, 1973), and also includes shared language, narrative and codes (Nahapiet and Ghoshal, 1998).

We find it useful to address Nahapiet and Ghoshal's (1998) argument that knowledge is created through two generic processes: exchange and combination. Specifically, we will later argue in terms of the conditions for exchange and combination they suggest, which are: opportunity – determined by accessibility to the objectified and collective forms of social knowledge; value expectancy – participants must expect the deployment to create value; motivation – participants must feel that their engagement will be worth their while, and combination capability – the capability to combine information and experience.

Collective Knowing in the Agora and Policy Learning

The concept we will use in the case discussion is *collective knowing*. We define collective knowing as a capability, a learned pattern of collective action, where the actors in the agora systematically modify their actions over time, through the learning process in the agora. Collective knowing is a capability that can only develop over time between actors who regularly meet and interact with each other. It is a capability for knowledge in action. This is pursued through dialogue between different actors. Through dialogue, theoretical concepts, discourses and real-life situations connect to create a mutual foundation for action and change a given situation in territory. In the agora, theoretical concepts are contested and made actionable. Dialogue is a means to create changes in language, behaviour, and organisational and institutional settings.

In our opinion, the concept in RIS literature that best connects with this approach to collective knowing is *policy learning*. Policy learning is social learning in communities or networks (Bennett and Howlett, 1992) that develops in the process of defining policy.

In territorial complexity, asymmetries of knowledge and information play a central role because policy makers operate with multiple objectives and one cannot expect the resulting policies to be independent of the learning process (Metcalfe, 1994). Our main argument about policy learning from this perspective is that in most territorial complexity situations there is no right solution that will come deductively from theory (Nauwelaers and Wintjes, 2008). However, there are expectations in many policy processes that there is some maximising, rationally right solution to problems, and research is sometimes expected to give the 'right' solution that should be implemented. We propose that inductive experimentation is also needed to find solutions in each specific case (Aranguren and Larrea, 2011). Such experimentation helps the development of individual and collective capabilities, linking action to concepts and theories.

We have decided to use the term *collective knowing* in the agora, and not policy learning in the agora, because we see that the first is not restricted exclusively to those agoras defined as policy networks. However, in the cases we discuss, the collective knowing has mostly materialised in policy learning processes where cyclical reflection and action on policy took place.

Case: Ezagutza Gunea, Part 3

In 2007 EG made an agreement with Orkestra, the Basque Institute of Competitiveness, to test a version of Porter's (1998) methodology for competitiveness diagnoses adapted to the Basque counties. The goal was that it should be used by local development agencies and other actors operating at county level to improve their strategies. EG was adequate for this as it gathered a diversity of actors that were considered relevant for competitiveness in local contexts.

The proposal from EG was to interpret the competitiveness diagnosis as a *process*, not as a *product* (Orkestra, 2008). In terms of the previous discussion about knowledge and knowing, the goal was to generate knowing out of a diagnosis that would initially be knowledge. To do so, a document was prepared by staff in EG together with researchers in Orkestra which presented and analysed the main indicators, reaching some conclusions on the situation in the county. For researchers, the process might have stopped there if the goal had not been established in terms of process. However, six work groups were then invited to explore how this product might be transformed into a process. Four of them represented the three subsystems in the RIS (two groups of firms: one of knowledge organisations and one of policy makers). Firms were divided into two groups due to the numbers involved. The first group included representatives with experience in EG, and the second newcomers to the network. The other two groups were composed on the one hand of EG staff, including a social researcher working for EG (Miren Larrea), and on the other of researchers from Orkestra who were not directly involved in the network.

Each group was asked to work with the diagnosis and construct a SWOT (Strengths, Weaknesses, Opportunities and Threats) analysis of the county. They were then asked to propose a sentence with a symbolic meaning of what they thought EG should be. In terms of the conflict/consensus discussion above, the goal was to explore potential conflict in the conception of the network itself, not in its specific activities. We were looking for conflicting positions regarding the goals of the agora, not the means. Participants declared afterwards that it had been a difficult exercise for them to think in those terms. There were moments during the process when the facilitators were afraid that nothing would come out of the discussion. However, it showed that although all participants except the external researchers were part of EG, there was no shared view on what EG should be. Every group finally reached an agreement on what their perspective was. Table 3.1 shows the sentences used by each of the groups.

Table 3.1   Sentences with the symbolic meaning of what EG should be

Group	Sentence: EG must ...
Academic group	... be the engagement for a win–win migration.
EG staff	... be energy for transformation, rooted in collaboration to compete in the world while strengthening the county.
Training centres	... be a county meeting point to activate society.
Policy makers	... be the soul of an innovative Iraurgi Hiria.*
Firms (newcomers)	... open the door to new paths.
Firms (experienced)	... be the wave that transforms hopes into realities.

*   Iraurgi Hiria was the name the county had been given in a prospective project led by the Provincial Council of Gipuzkoa called Gipuzkoa 2020, and was adopted by the local policy makers.

It is difficult to grasp what these sentences mean without knowing more about the discussions that took place. We present some extracts published in Navarro and Larrea (2007) that show the main ideas.

The newcomer firms (less than two years in the network) saw the network as a chance to explore new paths. They felt at the threshold of something new, but they had no clear expectations. The following is a fragment of their discourse:

EG is an invitation to open doors that might now be closed at two levels. First, individuals must open our minds, open to new ways to think and see things; to new experiences ... we understand that training and knowledge make us freer .... EG must influence everybody in the organisations in the network and help them grow as human beings ... but the invitation is not only for individuals, but for organisations. Opening doors means to be ready to go out but also let others in, so that they can learn from our experience ....

(answers from firms that were newcomers)

The firm representatives who had more experience in the network (on average four years) saw EG at a critical stage, as they felt that for the past few years they had been constructing expectations, but now they needed to make them real. They needed action, and they expressed it in this way:

EG must reach the hearts of individuals, engaging them to the project. The main asset to do it is the sense of belonging to the county that is now emerging after years of interaction among actors. EG must be an idealist project, with a shared utopianist vision that guides the behaviour of participants .... But the only way to keep expectations is to obtain results ... that is why EG must be an entity that makes expectations true by mobilising the different actors in the county ... to do so, the network must have a strong structure and leadership from the town councils and the development agency. Because of their vision, they must assume as their own the expectations generated by the sense of belonging of the rest of the actors to the county. The wave is the strength that impulses forward, but it also means opportunities that come and go ... it is important to be able to take the wave, if not, the wave goes. It is like expectations, that once generated have their time and if they are not transformed into realities they cannot be recovered.

(answers from firms with previous experience in EG)

Firms with a longer trajectory were saying that the four years of collaboration had created in them expectations of a county project that should be led by policy makers. But what was the perspective of such policy makers? In their reflection they included three elements. The first was Iraurgi Hiria (see note in Table 3.1). Their reflection was:

This concept adopted by the two town councils represents the political perspective of the county in the future .... It has been derived from the Gipuzkoa 2020 process to link the county level to the proposals made at the provincial level.

The second element was innovation:

> Gipuzkoa 2020 establishes four different scenarios and the Innovative
> Gipuzkoa is one of them. The innovative Iraurgi Hiria is the assimilation
> of this concept as a horizon for the county.

Finally, they added the following:

> EG is the soul of the innovative Iraurgi Hiria, the soul represents on the
> one hand the knowledge, which is intangible … and … on the other the
> spirit, which is the particular character of the county …
>
> (answers from the policy makers)

The third subsystem of the RIS – training centres in this case – had a more social
perspective than the other two subsystems. They said that:

> The definition of EG as a meeting point derives from the fact that this
> group feels out of the network, that mainly focuses on firms. In that
> sense, EG must be the meeting point for three worlds: politicians, the
> educational system and firms… this meeting point must generate in
> society a feeling of crisis… it must create the conscience in individuals
> of the need to change some values that are disarticulating society,
> engaging individuals with what is going on around them.
>
> (answers from the training centres)

The staff of EG mainly underlined the need to generate energy for change:

> Considering EG is based on two intangible concepts, knowledge and
> trust … they must be used as constructive energy …. EG transforms
> individual energy into a collective one … the collective energy must
> reach to individuals and teams making the move towards new forms of
> understanding of the reality surrounding them.
>
> (answers from EG staff, including one of the authors of this book)

Finally, the academic team played their role as outsiders, making engagement
one of the key issues. They argued that:

> EG means compromise with a project … the first requirement for that
> is that the members of the group recognise themselves as a group and
> understand that the links among them are strong enough to develop

> *a project together ... such project is a project of migration ... from a*
> *county based on traditional resources to one based on innovation ...*
> *this is a collective migration.*
>   *(answers from Orkestra researchers, outsiders to the EG process)*

Case Discussion: The Challenge of Collective Knowing

The process and reflections presented in the previous section took place at a moment when an explicit effort was being made to go from knowledge to knowing by taking the knowledge into action. The discussion will be divided into three phases. First, we will interpret what the contribution of different groups shows us about how social capital was developing in the group, second, we will discuss how the diversity of perspectives affects the development of collective knowing, and finally, we will discuss how all these reflections were taken into action, transforming knowledge into collective knowing.

THE INFLUENCE OF SOCIAL CAPITAL IN ACTION

Our main argument in this section is that collective knowing is the result of the construction of social capital in its different dimensions, and that such social capital is necessary for the social researcher who wants to contribute to collective knowing in the agora. Collective knowing is not the result of linear transfer of knowledge from those who know the answer to a problem to the ones who have the problem. If we consider that the role of the social researcher in the agora is to contribute to the development of collective knowing, and not to the accumulation of knowledge as stock, this poses certain challenges for social researchers.

In order to discuss these challenges, we begin with the contribution of researchers from Orkestra who had not been involved in processes with the actors. This group complemented the role of one of us (the authors), who was at the same time a researcher and part of the staff. For this process we integrated into the staff group. The research group had developed less social capital than the rest of the participants in the reflection process, as they had not been interacting with the members of EG. They were not part of the network (structural dimension), they lacked trust relationships with most participants (relational dimension), and they had not been part of the activity to develop a shared vision with the members (cognitive dimension). Their contribution was partly based on Porter's (1998) definition of the different stages of development of a country and previous research that concluded that the Basque Country had the challenge of evolving from the stage based on investment to the one based on innovation. This was knowledge for the members of the network. Their other argument, the one related to compromise, was based on the process approach to networks and clusters, where identity and compromise are critical elements. The contribution of the researchers was very consistent. We view it as knowledge, but this knowledge was not linked to action in EG.

We can compare this with the contribution of one of the groups that had developed more social capital in the EG process, the one composed of the firm representatives with a longer trajectory. Their organisations were part of the network, and they had personally represented them for some years. In addition, most of them had been or were at that time members of the management board, so they had interacted not only with other firm representatives in the network, but with policy makers and representatives of training centres too. This also meant that they had been at the core of decision making (structural dimension). They knew each other personally. Some of them had not known each other before entering the network, but for four years they had participated together in multiple meetings and workshops which had helped build trust (relational dimension). The fact that they were able to elaborate the arguments presented here and agree on what they were sharing shows that they had developed, at least to a certain extent, a shared vision of EG based on practice and interaction with the other members (cognitive dimension).

Both groups (the researchers and the firm representatives) had presented two critical issues. One was the need for change, and the other the need for compromise. Researchers were presenting it from a theoretical perspective, and practitioners were reaching the same conclusion from their practice in the agora (EG). The researchers did not have the social capital required to transform their knowledge into collective knowing. Firm representatives had the structure, trust and shared vision to shape action. We now simplify this by saying that both were knowledge, but the proposal by firms had a higher potential to be taken into action and thus transformed into collective knowing.

RELATING DIFFERENT KNOWING

By introducing the concept of territorial complexity, we discussed the diversity of conflicting perspectives and visions in the agora in Chapter 2. The goal is to overcome conflict. This is not done by homogenising perspectives, but by learning to integrate different perspectives into action. Collective knowing is not about having the right knowledge – the one everybody should accept – but about the capacity to combine the different knowing and knowledge of the participants in order to shape action.

To see this, the reaction of policy makers to the question of what EG should be is relevant. Their proposal was linked to action and based on social capital, but they focused on action and social capital not at the county level, where EG was acting, but at provincial level. This was probably the result of innovation policy not being considered an issue for politicians at municipal and county level, but for those acting at regional level. That might be why they conceptualised EG as a tool to materialise policies coming from higher levels of government, but not as a tool to have a county approach to innovation. This was in sharp contrast to what firm representatives were demanding from them when they said:

> The main asset … is the sense of belonging to the county that is now emerging after years of interaction among actors. … [T]he network must have a strong structure and leadership from the town councils and the development agency that because of their vision, must assume as their own the expectations generated by the sense of belonging to the county.

If we reflect in terms of social capital, we see that policy makers had also been part of the network and they were on the management board (structural dimension). They had good personal relationships with other actors, they knew each other, and they met not only in EG, but also in other contexts related to their role as policy makers (relational dimension). They agreed among themselves on their proposal of what EG should be, so they had a shared vision of this (cognitive dimension), but their vision was clearly divergent from that of firms.

They showed a stronger vision of how EG should connect to other policy levels than of what EG should be in the county or for its members. In terms of the conditions for exchange and combination presented by Nahapiet and Ghoshal (1998), the expectations of firm representatives and policy makers were divergent, not only in their expectations of what the network should be, but in their expectations of each other.

In our understanding of the role of social capital in the creation of collective knowing, there was no alignment in the cognitive dimension of social capital between firms and policy makers. This hindered the transformation of knowledge into collective knowing. The challenge for a social researcher who wanted to play a role in the generation of collective knowing was to contribute to adjusting such expectations and constructing a shared vision that could align policy makers and firm representatives in the pursuit of what all of them thought EG should be.

TAKING KNOWLEDGE TO ACTION: CREATING COLLECTIVE KNOWING

We have described a situation in which different positions and knowledge had been shared, some coming from experience, others coming from an academic analysis of the data. In order to illustrate diversity, we have mainly focused on researchers, the firms and policy makers with long experience in EG. But there were more elements in this diversity. The newcomer firms had their own approaches: they had less social capital and consistently showed a more individualistic approach to learning. They came to learn for their firm, and were not talking about a county (collective) project. Training centres argued that the network had not been able to integrate them into the process, which showed a weakness in the structural dimension of social capital. They were also asking for a more social approach to EG, widening the focus from an exclusively economic perspective.

Our argument is that often what researchers see is a snapshot based on explicit data (in this case, the report used to make the competitiveness diagnosis), and from that, by using our analytical frameworks, we give recommendations. We do not explore deeply the diversity of approaches, knowledge and knowing of the actors involved. So how can the contribution of researchers connect to the collective knowing that shapes action in the agora? We think that when, as researchers, we analyse a situation from the outside without a process of generation of social capital, we can do little more than what the outside research team had done. They had a consistent perspective on the issue. What they had said was perceived as sound by other actors, but they were not in a position to make the process evolve further. They were not part of the network, and they had no trust relationships except with the researcher who was part of the staff. After delivering the recommendations, the project was over for them.

But we were participating with the staff, and were in a different position. We were part of the network, we had built trust with the participants in the network and had been part of the efforts to construct a shared vision, although the process had shown that different groups still had different perspectives on what EG should be. We were still part of the process of taking knowledge into action, the process of constructing collective knowing. From this position we can connect the reflections of participants with a series of events that happened later.

The reflections made in the process were combined with a strategic reflection process developed in EG throughout 2005–2006 that was led by the management board and facilitated by staff, including the social researcher. The mission of EG was redefined in this process. One of the meaningful changes was that a specific challenge was defined for every type of actor participating (firms, policy makers, training centres). The challenge for policy makers was defined as 'participating in the process beyond funding it'. It is difficult to establish direct cause–effect relationships in social processes, and it is difficult to make an explicit connection between the discussions described above and this decision. But everybody on the board participated in both processes (the previously described diagnosis and the strategic reflection), and the demand from firms for more leadership from policy makers had an impact by posing the challenge to policy makers of having more involvement in the process than just contributing with funds.

In order to materialise this demand, a new work group was created in EG with the goal of exploring the role of town councils and local development agencies in innovation policy. It was an unusual approach in the Basque Country, where most assumed that innovation policy was the role of regional governments. The group was formed by the staff of EG, two policy makers and us (the social researcher). We started to explore the multi-level approach to innovation policy which claimed a role for local authorities in innovation policy that was complementary to regional policies. The first proposal for the creation of what finally became the Loiola Foundation (Figure 2.2 in Chapter 2), was made in this group in 2008. Knowledge was starting to be transformed into collective knowing a year after the different groups had reflected on what EG should be. As we saw in Chapter 2, three more years were needed before the foundation began to operate.

THE CHALLENGE OF RELAY OF COLLECTIVE KNOWING IN THE AGORA

In 2012, five years after the process described in this chapter, a new reflection process with policy makers was launched in EG. There had been a change in elected politicians as a result of elections. The crisis was hitting the county hard, and a discussion was held on how to face this. The role of EG in the county was discussed again. One of the politicians who had been in the municipal government at the time of the process described above was now in the opposition. He spoke, saying: 'We learnt about these issues some years ago, now we should use that knowledge.' He had the previous experience of having transformed knowledge into collective knowing, and was reacting to a debate where everything seemed to be starting all over again. Probably the only ones who understood what he meant were those who had shared the previous process (the director of the development agency, staff of EG and the social researcher). His claim was an attempt to keep the collective knowing alive at a time when there had been a change in the political leadership of the project. His claim helped to demonstrate that no matter how many documents are written and how well documented a process is, what keeps collective knowing in the agora are the people who shared the experience of action. The knowledge was there for the incoming politicians, as every process had been carefully documented in EG. But it was not until they had their own experience in EG, and thus transformed knowledge into knowing through action, that their own understanding of EG developed. Territorial development does not depend only on the linear transfer of knowledge. This is part of it, but not all. It is also necessary to construct social capital to transform such knowledge into knowing, and this requires the actors participating in the agora to take knowledge to action.

This situation described in 2012 shows the vulnerability of processes like EG, which are based on the construction of collective knowing, when there is a change in participants representing different organisations. The survival of the process depends on the ability of the participants to share the collective knowing to integrate the newcomers into the process. The role of the facilitators, mentioned in previous chapters, is critical to this. They are usually the ones who start the dialogue with the newcomers.

But the challenges are not only for the facilitators of policy networks and agoras. If constructing social capital is part of generating collective knowing, social researchers who want to contribute to agoras for territorial development face the challenge of integrating social capital as part of their research process.

Closing Comments

In order to share our final reflections on this chapter, we return to the statements by the firm representative of EG ('When we started I came here to see what I could get out of this for my firm. Nowadays I come because I want my children to have a future in this county') and the politician from EG ('We learnt about these issues some years ago, now we should use that knowledge'). They show that the transformation of knowledge into collective knowing is a long-term process that has little to do with the researcher giving the 'right answer' to policy makers. It has to do with how researchers dialogue with actors and influence the way they perceive territorial development. The researcher needs time and trust relationships in order to help develop collective knowing. The goal is to contribute concepts and frameworks to a discussion that in the long term will lead to action. But, as we have said, the goal is not to work with the actors in the process in order to make them understand and implement what the researchers consider is the right answer. The goal is to be able to integrate the researcher's contribution as one more perspective in a set of divergent approaches to the same issue. This contribution should help to amalgamate the different approaches into a collective capability linked to action.

This is one of the critical lessons from our experience of working with actors. When, as researchers, we got involved in processes that had the creation of a shared vision as a goal, we felt tempted to understand that our role was first to give the right answer to the problem, then to try to work with the actors to 'convince' them to implement the recommendation we were making. Experiences like the one in EG have shown us that our opinion as researchers, though very much respected by the actors, is just one more opinion among many. It can shape processes in one direction or another. But it should not do this by trying to homogenise perspectives to fit our own, but by being part of the diversity of perspectives as one more voice, helping actors to understand how the different perspectives can be channelled into action. That is why we insist that although for us a shared vision is a critical element in making territorial development happen, a shared vision has to do with making diversity actionable and not with homogenising the way different actors perceive territorial development.

In order to handle diversity, researchers need to understand the meanings, motivations and expectations of the actors, and this can only be done if there is social capital. Agoras are thus not spaces for knowledge transfer from researchers to the rest of the actors, but spaces where new knowing is generated through the combination of different types of knowledge and knowing.

But the perspective of researchers on their own role in the agora is not the only relevant one. In order to develop collective knowing, policy makers must see the researcher not only as a source of data, reports or the right answers to their problems, but as a partner in the policy process – an ally in pursuit of some goals, and a critical voice in pursuit of others. The transformation of knowledge into collective knowing requires the facilitation of a long-term process that can overcome elections and changes in governments. Social researchers can contribute to keeping the process going, but in order to do so, policy makers must accept researchers as process facilitators throughout the whole policy process. This role of the researchers as facilitators who sometimes create questions and do not always have the answers poses some challenges to researchers. In a conversation in which we presented our approach to a fellow researcher, we talked about the times when we had to face policy makers without having the answers, and when we had even participated in processes where it had taken almost a year to build an agreement among actors about what the problem was. He asked whether we were worried that policy makers might think we were not good researchers because we were explicit about not having the answers for such a long time. He was right; it was not easy to find policy makers who understood policy learning in the way we did. In Part II we will propose an approach to research that we feel can help both researchers and policy makers to face these challenges.

PART II

Action Research, Mode 2 Knowledge, Cogeneration and Pluralism

Part II builds on the argument that in order to play the role we propose for social researchers in territorial development, we need to approach knowledge generation in Mode 2 – or as we interpret it from an action research perspective, knowledge cogeneration (Chapter 4). We propose pluralistic environments for action research as adequate contexts for cogeneration of knowledge (Chapter 5).

We had been working in different territorial development projects for a long time before we knew about the concepts of action research, Mode 2 and pluralism. As practitioners, we did not reflect much on how we were working together with other actors in the territory, including researchers. We took it for granted that the way we were working was how we should work together. When we were working as researchers, we adapted to the dominant mode of knowledge production. But we felt we were not generating the change we expected and began to question our own taken-for-granted assumptions about how we were working together with territorial actors and how we were generating knowledge. In this part of the book we reflect on the difference between the action researcher as facilitator of a knowledge generation process and the action researcher as a cogenerator of knowledge in the agora. It is a fine line between these two positions, and we will explore this in Chapter 4.

Innovation and change are often generated by new combinations of knowledge, as Schumpeter (1968) argued. Action research is a process where researchers and practitioners with different kinds of knowing work together, but it takes time to build pluralistic action research environments in which researchers with different kinds of knowing can work together. In the following chapters in Part II, we will explore in depth our own change in knowledge cogeneration over a long time perspective.

4

Change in Research Practice
for Territorial Development

In 1999 a PhD project about a typology of local production systems was presented in the Basque Country. The PhD student had been educated in an approach to research where the researcher was supposed to remain neutral and distant from the object of analysis. She had used secondary data produced by the regional statistics institute to analyse 13 production systems, and grouped them in a way that could help to adjust policy to the specificities of each system. The work was published in a book by the Basque Government in 2000 and sent to the main policy making actors in the region. She never received any feedback from any of the virtual readers of the book. During the writing process there had been no connection at all between the territorial actors and the researcher. She had never talked to the policy makers for whom she had written the recommendations. In 2002 she left her position at a university to go to work in a local development agency where she could use her knowledge in practice.

The researcher had not reflected on these facts until she started to write with a Norwegian action researcher in 2009. He had finished his PhD about the regional role of universities in 2007. In his PhD he introduced action research as 'an approach which is looked upon with scepticism within the academic community because of its methodology based on participation with practitioners' (Karlsen, 2007, p. 58). Still, he continued:

> *I have chosen action research (AR) as my main method for data generation. AR rests on the ethos of participation with practitioners. As a participant the action researcher has the potential to acquire a holistic picture of the process rather than partial perspectives represented by most other methods.*
>
> *(Karlsen, 2007, p. 59)*

These two PhDs, which reflect radically different approaches to research for territorial development, are our own PhDs. Both are part of our experience, and important milestones in the thread leading to this book.

Our change process, from 1999 when the first PhD was written to 2013 when this book is being written, has inspired this chapter. This process has responded to a complex combination of personal decisions and organisational arrangements of many people and organisations. It would be impossible to show all of them in this discussion. In pursuit of the aim of writing inside out, what we will do is analyse some critical steps from change processes in which we have participated. There is no generalisability of the process. But we believe that the challenges we faced and the discussion of the processes we lived through might be useful for other researchers who want to change their role in agoras for territorial development.

There are two main frameworks that have helped us to develop the discussion presented in this chapter. One is related to the concepts of Mode 1 and Mode 2 of knowledge production (Gibbons et al., 1994). It is difficult to make complex processes fit into clear frameworks. Among the different contributions we have analysed, this is the one that could most clearly help analyse the differences in the approaches of the two PhDs previously presented and the change process since them. The second framework is the cogenerative action research model of Greenwood and Levin (2007), which is the framework that has had most influence on our understanding of how participation with policy makers can take place in the agora. It is a critical contribution to our own framework of how to construct a Mode 2 environment for territorial development, which we present at the end of this chapter. In this way, we make AR our approach to Mode 2.

The case study and discussion show part of the change process we have gone through by participating in different teams and organisations, all related to research and territorial development. Through the different phases, the evolution is described from a detached mode of knowledge production towards a cogenerative process of knowledge generation in the context of application – that is, in the agora.

This chapter has two main goals. The first is to help researchers who come from a position of detachment from the actual change processes of policy makers and want to experiment with a cogenerative approach of participation in processes. The main conclusion is that it is not exclusively a matter of the researcher's personal choice which can be taken into practice from one day to the next. It takes a long time and considerable effort, as the people in the research organisations (universities and research centres) as well as in policy-oriented organisations (governments and their agencies) must change routines and behaviour that are deeply rooted.

The second goal is to share our understanding of Mode 2 agoras for territorial development. In this case, our conclusion is that there is no static model of a Mode 2 agora. What we share here are some thoughts on how the interaction between policy makers and researchers takes place from a dynamic perspective.

In order to fulfil these goals, the chapter will begin by presenting the main concepts used, mostly related to the Mode 1–Mode 2 discussion and the cogenerative model for AR. As a case, we present our own change process from Mode 1 to Mode 2. The discussion will focus on what the critical elements were in making this change possible and how we can describe our understanding of Mode 2 agoras nowadays. The chapter will end with closing comments on some differences between the cogenerative model and our approach.

THE MODE 1–MODE 2 FRAMEWORK IN SOCIAL SCIENCES

The Mode 1–Mode 2 discussion presented by Gibbons et al. (1994) is not the only framework which proposes an approach to learning that is developed in interaction. Some approaches that have been discussed in the innovation system literature are the DUI (Doing, Using, Interacting) mode of innovation (see Jensen et al., 2007), and the combined and complex mode of innovation (CCI; see Isaksen and Karlsen, 2012a). They propose an interactive approach to learning in the innovation system, but they do not explicitly pose the challenge for researchers to interact with practitioners.

The Mode 1 and Mode 2 concepts were much discussed when they were first suggested by Gibbons et al. (1994), and they are still influential. In Mode 1, knowledge is constructed in specific disciplinary environments (Gibbons et al., 1994). This process makes the knowledge more general, and it can suit more than one purpose. When the knowledge construction process is finished, it is transferred to the users through an invention, a theory, a scientific article, a PhD thesis or a report. However, the challenge is that the knowledge is not ready for use in any context since it is abstract and decontextualised. In Mode 2 scientific, technological and industrial creations become closely connected (Gibbons et al., 1994). The main argument from the authors is that in Mode 2, knowledge is produced in a context of application in the agora. This implies that the process of knowledge creation and the use of knowledge have been integrated; it has become the same. The authors argue that knowledge is created through intense dialogue between different constructors and users of knowledge. The context of application describes the total environment in which scientific problems arise, methodologies are developed, outcomes are disseminated and uses are defined. Table 4.1 compares the two modes.

We do not want to emphasise the differences between Mode 1 and Mode 2, but instead will focus on the Mode 2 agora. Gibbons et al. (1994, p. 37) relate Mode 2 to *hybrid fora* where communities are composed of people who have been socialised in different subsystems, disciplines or working environments, but who subsequently learn different styles of thought, modes of behaviour, knowledge and social competence that they did not originally possess. In a later work, these authors give the definition of agora that we have used in this book (see Nowotny et al., 2001). We interpret this concept of hybrid fora as an approach to what they later defined as agora.

Both Mode 1 and Mode 2 approach problem solving, but there is a contrast between problem solving which is carried out following the codes of practice relevant to a particular discipline (Mode 1) and problem solving which is organised around a particular application (Mode 2). In Mode 2, knowledge is always produced in a context of continuous negotiation, and it will not be produced unless and until the interests of the various actors around a particular application are included (Gibbons et al., 1994, p. 3). This is a feature of agoras for territorial development.

Table 4.1   Comparison of Mode 1 and Mode 2

Mode 1	Mode 2
Knowledge is created within the context of an academic community	Knowledge is created in a context of application
Knowledge is created in a disciplinary mode	Knowledge is created in a transdisciplinary mode
Homogeneous knowledge is required	Heterogeneous knowledge is used
Hierarchical organisation of knowledge production	Heterarchical, flexible and transient organisation
Quality control through peer review	Quality control carried out by the participants in the knowledge creation process through social accountability

Source: Adapted from Karlsen (2007, p. 37), based on Gibbons et al. (1994).

When Gibbons et al. (1994) present the Mode 1–Mode 2 concepts, they recognise that although their scope is not only science and technology but also social sciences and humanities, they devote more attention to the former than to the latter. When they define the agora (Nowotny et al., 2001) and approach the discussion of social change, the concrete procedures for interaction in the agora remain a black box. But although the issue is not discussed in depth, Gibbons et al. (1994, p. 105) make reference to the detachment of social researchers. They argue that in order to maintain their analytic and technical posture, the social sciences have generally tried to maintain a style of reflexivity which links with contextualisation in a consciously detached manner. In contrast with the humanities, the social sciences attempt to stay intellectually aloof from the creation of values and signification. The discussion in this chapter aims to contribute to the debate about how Mode 2 can be developed in social sciences and, more concretely, in territorial development.

ACTION RESEARCH AND KNOWLEDGE COGENERATION PROCESSES

In their proposal of the cogenerative action research model Greenwood and Levin (2007) argue that an AR process can be initiated only when there is a common agreement among actors (the 'problem owners' or the 'insiders') to do so and to invite 'outsiders' into the process. While the insiders own the problem, outsiders are the professional researchers/external change agents who seek to facilitate a co-learning process aimed at solving the problem and at the same time contributing to the scientific discourse. Greenwood and Levin (2007) present two main differences between insiders and outsiders. One is that most insiders have to live directly with the results of any change activity in the project, whereas most outsiders can leave. Another difference is that the insiders have the central influence on what the focus of the research activity should be.

This distinction between insiders and outsiders is developed mostly in the context of workplace research and organisational change (see also Klev and Levin, 2012). Figure 4.1 reproduces what we name in this book as the *cogenerative model* following Greenwood and Levin (2007), which is named as *participatory change as cogenerative learning* by Klev and Levin (2012). In the discussion in this chapter we will argue for some alternative interpretations of the process we think can take place when taking the cogenerative model from workplace development to territorial development.

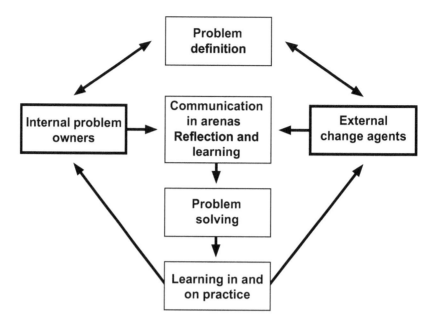

Figure 4.1   **Participatory change as cogenerative learning**

Source: Reproduced by permission of the publishers, adapted from R. Klev and M. Levin, *Participative Transformation: Learning and Development in Practising Change* (Farnham: Gower, 2012), p. 68. Copyright © 2012.

In the cogenerative model, AR is a cyclical process in which insiders interact with outsiders. Problem definition is the first step in a mutual learning process (Greenwood and Levin, 2007; Klev and Levin, 2012). The whole research process emerges from demands arising outside academia, but AR professionals do not blindly accept any problem formulation forwarded by the local participants.

The next step involves insiders and outsiders working together to communicate and create arenas (in our terminology, agoras) for mutual reflection and learning. The arena for communication between the groups of actors must be configured properly. It can be a meeting between two or more people, a team-building session, a search conference, a task force meeting, a leadership group meeting, a public community meeting etc. The key point is that an arena allows communicative actions to take place in an environment structured for cogenerative learning and research. Greenwood and Levin (2007) argue that although the outsiders do not have a formal position in the local organisational hierarchy, they exert influence through participant expectations that they will play a major role in designing and managing the change process.

The reflection process is followed by action by the insiders. Since the researchers are active participants in the process, the researchers get inside information about the process as the process is unfolding – that is, in real time.

By collaborating in a process, participants learn to reflect *in* and *on* action (Schön, 1983; Schön, 1987). It is important to design processes in which insiders and outsiders have stages or phases in which they reflect on their own before meeting again to define the next step in the knowledge cogeneration process related to a new problem definition. In this way, the process goes on cyclically until it comes to its end.

Case: Orkestra, Part 1[1]

The choice of a case for the discussion of the transition from Mode 1 to Mode 2 and the main features of Mode 2 in territorial development was not immediately evident. The case needed to show that such a transition involves multiple changes in a long-term process in which different organisations, teams and individuals are involved. But how to connect all these changes? The case could tell the story of multiple organisations and teams, but on their own none of them showed the complexity we feel defines a process of moving from Mode 1 to Mode 2. Since we had decided to write this book inside out, from our own experiences, we concluded that it was our own change trajectory that we could best analyse, trying to explain the main changes in organisations and research teams that shaped it. That is why we reflect on a thread in our experience that starts with the PhD completed by one of us in 1999 and ends with the writing of this book.

We have chosen some milestones in the change process and put them in a timeline (see Figure 4.2). In doing so, we do not wish to create a sense of linearity in the process. On the lower side, the timeline shows organisational arrangements we were part of and which pushed forward our learning process on Mode 2. On the upper side we have defined some phases in the learning process where praxis changed. The first of the PhD processes presented in the introduction to this chapter helped to characterise Mode 1 in Phase 1. The rest are phases where we partly developed our approach to Mode 2. The phases in the timeline are not as distinct as they seem and do not substitute for each other. Old processes continue to exist alongside new ones. Still, in the process there is an evolution that we could describe as a change from Mode 1 towards Mode 2 knowledge production. The figure is inspired by Karlsen et al. (2012).

---

1   Part 2 of the case is presented in Chapter 5.

We have participated in this process together with many other researchers and practitioners, but it is our perspective on the change process that we describe. The sequence itself and the choice of the facts included in Figure 4.2 are the result of our learning process and our interpretation. Finally, even though the process is based on our experiences, we intend to have a discussion that is of more general interest.

The main features of each of the phases regarding modes of knowledge generation, the main research approaches and outcomes are described in the following paragraphs.

During Phase 1 we developed our research on local development in a university research team without contact with the local actors. We developed conceptual models related to local development that were adapted to the context of the Basque Country, and used secondary data to test them. We published in academic journals and had reports published by different institutions in the Basque Country, but there was no feedback from local actors (Larrea, 1999; Larrea, 2000a; Larrea, 2000b; Larrea, 2000c; Larrea, 2003). This is what we have called *linear knowledge generation and transfer* in the timeline in Figure 4.2.

In 2002 we moved to EG, the network that was used as a case study in Part I of this book. EG became an agora where researchers and practitioners worked together, with specific problems detected in the development of the network. Researchers attained an in-depth understanding of the processes needed to create and develop networks for local development. Various publications in academic journals and edited books followed, with a more international coverage than in the previous phase (Parrilli et al., 2010; Navarro and Larrea, 2007; Larrea et al., 2010; Larrea et al., 2007; Iturrioz et al., 2006; Aranguren et al., 2007).

Figure 4.2   A transition from Mode 1 towards Mode 2 knowledge creation

What practitioners in EG were getting out of the cogenerative process were proposals for the design of the network, models to approach knowledge management in the network, strategies to incorporate small firms in the network, diagnoses of competitiveness for the county, and strategies for innovation policies that they took into action in the EG context. We have called this phase *focused experimental cogeneration*.

Then we moved back to the university environment (the University of Deusto), but this time to a very specific organisation working with a high level of autonomy from the departmental structure, Orkestra, the Basque Institute of Competitiveness. Orkestra was a context that made it possible to take cogeneration to a system level, giving a name to Phase 3 in the timeline in Figure 4.2.

In order to do so, an agreement was signed between Orkestra and Garapen, the association of county development agencies in the Basque Country, to develop knowledge cogeneration processes open to all local development agencies that required support in their local networking processes. In this way, knowledge was cogenerated not only in a specific county network, but with average thirteen county networks in the Basque Country. Knowledge cogeneration gained scope, but each network did not go into in-depth AR processes as EG had. Various papers and articles were a reflection of this phase (for example, Larrea et al., 2012; Karlsen et al., 2012; Aranguren et al., 2010a; Aranguren et al., 2010b). The cogenerative process offered practitioners competitiveness analyses, cluster maps and network development proposals for their specific territories that they used in their own processes. It also helped to strengthen awareness of the role they could play in the innovation system of the Basque Country.

Due, among other things, to our experience of county-level processes, we were invited to develop AR processes in networks at provincial and regional levels. One of them was Gipuzkoa Sarean (GS), which is presented in Part III of the book. Consequently a series of projects developed in Orkestra that involved networks at different levels (municipal/county, province and region) that shared learning processes. The territorial complexity grew compared to the previous context of exclusively local actors, and again the AR approaches for cogeneration were challenged. Power play and political processes, together with shared leadership, emerged as key issues (Aranguren and Larrea, 2011; Karlsen and Larrea, 2012). We were involved in more strategic processes for the development of the territory. The main results for policy makers were spaces for policy learning. This is the phase we labelled *multi-level knowledge cogeneration*.

We believe that every step in the timeline brought us to a different phase of Mode 2, which means that there is no single approach to Mode 2 agoras. We also acknowledged that we could not understand the change process of researchers without understanding the change (as reflection, learning, decisions and actions) in other territorial actors, such as network managers and policy makers at local, provincial and regional levels. In the following discussion we explore these issues more deeply.

Case Discussion: The Development of Agoras for Territorial Development

CHALLENGING NORMATIVE APPROACHES

The PhD presented in 1999 and its approach to research was the result of different kinds of influences. We focus now on the specific institutional setting in that university environment and how it defined what a PhD should be like. First, neutrality was a goal. The researcher was an observer who should not get involved in the phenomenon being analysed, to avoid influencing it. Second, research was a rational process, and emotions were never mentioned. Third, it was safer to have a dissertation with quantitative data and statistical analysis. Finally, the research question should be derived from the literature review and what other authors considered was lacking in academia. The PhD process met all of these conditions. We had no awareness of following any normative approach, as the rules of the game responded to *what research was*. We positioned the PhD in relation to content, linking the research to the Italian approach to industrial districts, but saw no need to position it in relation to how knowledge was generated. We were taking this approach for granted in 1999.

Fourteen years later, this book on territorial development and action research follows quite different criteria. We assume that it is not possible to reflect on the issues we are writing about while keeping a neutral position. We understand that emotions have played a role as critical as that of rational approaches in the change process studied. We are writing using experience as data – not just the experiences of others, but mainly our own experiences. Finally, the research questions behind our arguments have been derived from real-life problems posed by territorial actors.

We were initially tempted to argue that we had a normative approach in 1999 that led us to understand research in an uncritical way. We then went through a process of questioning such a normative approach, and evolved towards another that was the result of our critical thinking. We soon realised that it is hard to argue that the approach in this book is less normative than the one we had in 1999, though the things we are taking for granted now are not the same ones we took for granted at that time.

When talking about the research and knowledge cogeneration process, the contribution of researchers to academia, the roles of insiders and outsiders, the need for agoras for dialogue and the relevance of democratic dialogue, we are replicating normative approaches mainly inherited from the pragmatic approach of action research.

It would be a mistake not to make this approach explicit and to take it for granted that what we are doing now is the 'right way' to do it. It is important for researchers to advance in awareness of the normative discourses by which we are affected. We need to avoid the temptation of believing we are not affected by any and that the rules of the game we follow are neutral.

Our main argument related to normative approaches in this change process is not that we are less normative now. The argument is that due to the continuous need to reflect in and on action in the processes we are developing, we are now more aware of such normative approaches than we were at the beginning of the timeline. We find that this is a strength of AR when trying to develop Mode 2 agoras.

In our case, awareness of the possibility of conducting research in a different way was not provoked by reading about a pragmatic approach to action research, but by our experiences as practitioners. The will to change from Mode 1 knowledge creation emerged from the combination of two circumstances in EG: the need we had as practitioners to solve real problems, and the fact that our capabilities at that time were research capabilities which we had previously developed. Our experience was that when we were at a distance from the university environment, we could see the possibility of approaching research in a different way. We do not mean that it is impossible to change while embedded in the university system. But for us it was more difficult to be aware of the normative approaches we were taking for granted. That is why in the next section we will reflect on some normative discourses held by territorial actors that played a role in helping us to see our own normative discourses.

EZAGUTZA GUNEA: AN UNINTENDED CREATION OF MODE 2

Ezagutza Gunea, which we analysed from a territorial development perspective in Part I, was not the result of an explicit intention to create a Mode 2 environment. In the process of hiring staff for the network, one of the candidates (us) happened to be a researcher. The conversations held with the director of the development agency showed that they thought that, 'having someone coming from a university would be good for the project'.

There was not only a normative discourse on research at the university, there was a normative discourse on territorial development in EG. At that time the main discourses on territorial development were arguing for new modes of governance, participatory approaches and a more active role for universities in regions. In our case, it was the normative discourse on territorial development and the desire of practitioners to have a university that added value to territorial development that pushed our way to AR. Without having heard about the cogenerative model of Greenwood and Levin (2007), a few researchers at the university and practitioners in the network started to cogenerate knowledge.

The integration of a researcher in the development network led some policy makers to worry that the discussion would become too theoretical. An explicit assertion of the need for the creation of a language that would be adapted to firm, training centre and town council representatives was made to us. It was a slow process of mutual knowing and shaping to define a work method for EG that integrated, in a natural way, contributions from the territorial actors and researchers.

When telling a story, it is helpful to have a well-defined argument about a clear strategy and strong leadership. But there was no explicit strategy for Mode 2 in this case. Only a series of circumstances and small decisions (more or less conscious) that led to the development of AR as an approach to Mode 2. Intertwined with these small decisions was the normative approach for a more active role for a university in territorial development. Our conclusion on this phase is that agoras can develop even in situations where there is no clearly defined strategy to create them and without having an explicit claim on Mode 2.

ORKESTRA: MODE 2 AS A STRATEGY FOR CHANGE

The second organisation that was critical in the change process is Orkestra, the research institute where we (the authors) work together at the time of writing this book. In this case, the approach to Mode 2 was more straightforward, though implicit. Its foundational documents stated that Orkestra was created to 'influence the real competitiveness of the Basque Country'. This meant that it was created not only to conduct research from the outside and observe competitiveness, but to change it. This approach was confirmed in the constitution of an administration board on which regional governments, firms and the university were represented. It could be classified among the new institutional arrangements, linking government and industry, that emerge in Mode 2 (Gibbons et al., 1994).

So there was a clearer discourse on the change that was pursued than in EG, and it fitted into the Mode 2 discourse. But when the institute started to operate in 2006, staffed mainly by researchers from the university, the initial design of the research programme was quite Mode 1. Although the discourse was in place, change was not automatic. Among other contributions, the experience with EG was used to adapt research approaches to the mission. We do not claim that Orkestra is a Mode 2 organisation, nor that AR is the main approach in Orkestra. But there is a space for these perspectives in the search for such adaptation.

One of the strategies followed by the management of Orkestra was the recruitment of several people with mixed profiles linking research and practice in local development agencies or technology centres. Co-operation agreements were also signed with an array of actors in the regional innovation system.

One difference between this agora and EG is its structural link to the university. Although some of the entrepreneurs who created Orkestra were former policy makers and were linked to relevant firms in the territory, from the beginning they worked together with the university and researchers in the pursuit of its creation. We could interpret Orkestra as an agora for Mode 2 in the context of a university, but with a critical role played by practitioners.

GARAPEN AND GIPUZKOA SAREAN: THE CONSCIOUS CREATION OF AGORAS

Unlike the previous examples of Ezagutza Gunea and Orkestra, the projects with the association of local development agencies in the Basque Country (Garapen) and the Gipuzkoa Sarean project with the provincial council of Gipuzkoa are the result of explicit agreements between researchers and practitioners to work using AR principles and with a Mode 2 approach.

None of this would have been possible without the learning process both in EG and Orkestra, nor would the formal context for starting the projects have existed if Orkestra had not consolidated an approach to research favourable to Mode 2.

Both projects (described in the last phases of the timeline) might seem to follow the pattern proposed by Gibbons et al. (1994, p. 9) of less firmly institutionalised contexts for knowledge creation. People come together in temporary work teams and networks which dissolve when a specific learning process is developed. But our experience differs from this perspective in two ways. On the one hand, we believe that a long-term change process was needed before these specific projects could start working with AR. Our reflection is that there might be a light institutionalisation of Mode 2 in terms of specific projects. But in order to develop these specific projects, there are institutions (organisations as well as rules of the game) that need to change. We argue that a deep institutional change is required in the territory in order to generate the context for such light institutionalisation in specific projects. On the other hand, we worked in the context of specific projects that generated temporary work teams. But the networks created between territorial actors and researchers have remained in the long term, becoming the context in which new projects emerge.

Evolving from Mode 1 to Mode 2 requires institutional change, which makes its development a difficult process. We have seen in previous sections that normative approaches can facilitate such change. But we have also gone through situations where there is a Mode 2 normative discourse and Mode 1 routines continue to dominate. There is a risk of changing discourses without really changing the institutional setting. We feel that Mode 2 is growing as a normative discourse in territorial development, but its actual development is far from achieved.

Collective Knowing in the Agora

Both the Mode 2 concept and the cogenerative AR model presented above have been useful for interpreting our experiences in the agora. Still, neither of them completely covers our interpretation of what goes on in the agora. That is why in this section we propose a framework of our own, based on the two previously discussed, but with distinct elements that we present now.

Gibbons et al. (1994) describe Mode 2, but the specific procedures needed to develop it in social sciences remain black-boxed. Besides, most researchers in territorial development in our environments have more experience in Mode 1 than in Mode 2. Consequently, even when reflecting from experience, we have a better understanding of the procedures in Mode 1 than in Mode 2.

With their cogenerative model, Greenwood and Levin (2007) open the black box of the process that explains what goes on between researchers and practitioners in the agora. But they present a role for the social researcher in workplace-based experiences. We reinterpret it in the context of territorial development. For Greenwood and Levin (2007), researchers mostly use their process knowledge, and participants bring knowledge about the problem the AR process seeks to solve. Our experience of the role of the researcher in territorial development is closer to what Johnsen and Normann (2004, pp. 226–7) describe when they talk about the six roles of the action researcher: the facilitator, the observer, the supplier, the participant, the bridge builder and the service provider. They argue that this list implies that the role of the action researcher is to be both an insider and an outsider to the practice field, which is in contrast with the clear-cut division between insiders and outsiders in the cogenerative model of Greenwood and Levin (2007).

One of the main lessons from the process described in the previous sections is that there are various circumstances that can make the researcher a territorial actor in the process. In EG, one of us was playing a research role but at the same time was the co-ordinator of a network – see Pettigrew (2003) for a very similar case. In the case of Orkestra, this research organisation is part of the RIS, so it is clearly one more actor in territorial development. This makes it very difficult for Orkestra researchers to be perceived as neutral in discussions about the RIS and territorial development. The distinction between insiders and outsiders in the cogenerative process is blurred. Greenwood and Levin (2007) argue that the outsider is not part of the hierarchical structure, but as we argued in Chapter 2, in a situation of territorial complexity this can be applied to all actors, who are interdependent but autonomous.

In this situation, our proposal is not to avoid the distinction between the roles of researchers and practitioners. We have found the distinction between insiders and outsiders useful when discussing our roles with policy makers. But we think that being a territorial actor is implicit in the role of the social researcher in agoras for territorial development. When the issue is territorial development, action researchers do not enter the agora to help solve the problem for insiders, they are often problem owners.

The multiplicity of roles of the action researcher also leads to discussion on the type of knowledge researchers contribute. Greenwood and Levin (2007) emphasise process knowledge:

> *AR competence involves learning a broad array of research techniques, work forms, and learning to manage or facilitate collaborative research processes and to assist in the process of documentation and synthesis of the results and action implications.*
>
> *(Greenwood and Levin, 2007, p. 101)*

In the long-term case described in this chapter, disciplinary field knowledge has been a critical contribution to the debate with actors. There were times, especially when AR was first used in Orkestra, when tensions were created within the research team when some researchers entered the discussion with policy makers not only in terms of the process, but also in terms of content related to territorial development. For those approaching the role of action researcher exclusively as a facilitator, there was a risk of researchers 'contaminating' what the practitioners were expressing in the process. This was an argument developed from within the AR team, but connected with the argument about the researcher not influencing the object of analysis. Sometimes, by emphasising the facilitator role, we stayed out of the knowledge cogeneration process with the participants, while facilitating knowledge cogeneration among them.

Our approach nowadays is that the researcher on territorial development has, besides experience based knowledge as territorial actor, both process and disciplinary field knowledge. Both are public goods that should contribute to the debate in the agora. When contributing with process knowledge, the social researcher facilitates the dialogue among others. When contributing with field knowledge, the researcher enters the dialogue as one more actor in the territory. This does not mean that the discourse is contaminated, as long as it is clear that what is expressed is one more approach to the issue, and not superior knowledge. If this is done, there is no manipulation of the process.

Consequently, we consider that the researcher entering an AR process in territorial development contributes with process knowledge, but also with experience-based (actor) knowledge and field (academic) knowledge. In writing this book, it has been difficult for us to disentangle one type of knowledge from another.

The consideration of social researchers as actors in territorial development also brings a different interpretation of problem definition in the cogenerative process. Greenwood and Levin (2007) argue that researchers must be invited into the AR process by practitioners. Our argument is that as actors in territorial development, it can be researchers who invite policy makers into an AR process. In the final phases of the process presented in the case (the timeline), we did this. It was the sense of being problem owners in the territory and the feeling of sharing a problem with policy makers that led us to initiate processes. We see this as related to what Eikeland (2006) describes as the 'nativeness' of the researcher when he talks about research:

> It ignores, and renders suspect the practical experiences of native performers, readers, thinkers, speakers and writers, or it is unable to attain to native experiences because it doesn't analyse its own nativeness, i.e. the prejudices, etc. of its own habitus. But nativeness cannot be eliminated from research. Research must go through native experience. Hence the validation and use of practical, personal experience must move from periphery to centre of any research process, transforming it in the moment.
>
> (Eikeland, 2006, pp. 209–10)

In Figure 4.3 we propose a framework for the cogenerative process in agoras for territorial development. It is inspired by Greenwood and Levin (2007) and Klev and Levin (2012), but mainly based on the differences with them shared in the previous discussions.

In this framework we have kept social researchers and policy makers as distinct figures with distinct roles in the agora, but we do not label them as insiders and outsiders. We argue that they contribute to the dialogue process with all the types of knowledge they have; this means that in the same way that researchers contribute with experience-based knowledge, policy makers bring theoretical concepts and frameworks into the discussion.

Greenwood and Levin's approach to problem definition is critical for the creation of collective knowing. It is the agreement on a problem that links researchers and practitioners in territorial development. When changing the framework for AR from workplace to territory, we argue that researchers on territorial development are also problem owners, and it is often part of their mission to contribute to such development. Reflection and action cycles on the agreed problem help to generate the collective knowing we defined in Chapter 3.

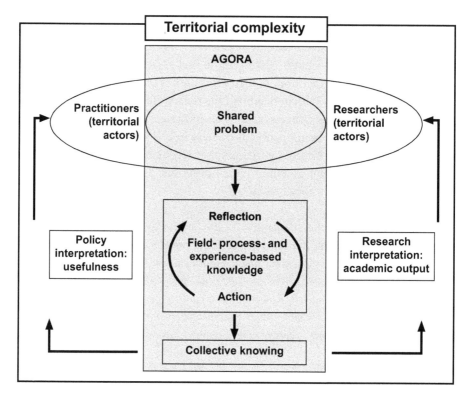

Figure 4.3   Creation of collective knowing in the agora

Closing Comments

In the previous section we presented our own approach to the cogenerative process in agoras for territorial development, inspired by Greenwood and Levin (2007). In order to do so, we discussed some elements that make their approach (workplace-oriented) and ours (territory-oriented) different. These are mainly the relevance of disciplinary knowledge and the nativeness of the researcher. In these closing comments we bring in an issue that has not been explicitly integrated into the previous discussion: our focus on change in research. When Greenwood and Levin (2007) argue that action research is a mutual learning process, we interpret this as their assuming that the researcher also changes. But while they make a strong argument about the change of practice by practitioners, they say less about how research and the researchers change due to the mutual learning. By basing our approach on our own experience, we have tried to make the researchers' change process more explicit. Such change is an important element in collective knowing.

By showing the timeline of our own change process, we wanted to underline this dimension of AR, which we find essential to understanding the role of researchers in territorial development. We feel that the role of researchers in a territory is not only to help practitioners change. It is also to change research, so that the capability to help actors in their change processes will improve. This requires making the change process of researchers explicit.

This can also be interpreted in the terms we previously presented by saying that researchers need to connect to their own nativeness. In this way, as natives, they are also part of the change process. Eikeland (2006, p. 219) argues that in some action research approaches the researchers participate in development processes among 'the natives', where researchers 'intervene'. The planned change and development processes are not among the researchers, but among the participants. Meanwhile, the participants are not invited into the researchers' change process. This process remains closed as a black box, even to other researchers.

It is in an effort to connect to such nativeness that we decided to write this book inside out. As researchers in territorial development, we want to contribute by finding the approaches to research that best fit with our goal of being actors in such development. Our own change process is the strongest instrument we have to generate change in other actors. But if we are not aware and explicit about our own change process, it will be hard to link both change processes. In Figure 4.3 this means that the process represented by the arrow on the right, in terms of the research interpretation of collective knowing in order to contribute to academia, should also include how research itself is changed by such collective knowing. This is seldom seen in academic output on RISs and territorial development, which mainly focuses on the change processes of other actors.

We will attempt to do this in Chapter 5, in which we explore our change process more deeply, focusing this time on our efforts to develop an AR environment in Orkestra.

5

Creating a Pluralistic Action Research Environment

In 2009 we made the decision to try to create an action research environment in Orkestra. This decision was initially made by an area co-ordinator and one researcher in an organisation in which nobody had been trained to be an action researcher. After some initial reflections, the following questions arose: Should the strategy be to concentrate on PhD training programmes to educate a new generation of action researchers? Would it be possible to create an AR environment with the teams that already constituted Orkestra?

We have met many researchers who have wanted to create conditions in their organisations that will allow them to have a bigger impact on territorial processes. In this chapter we use our experience to discuss critical elements in the creation of what we have called a pluralistic action research environment. To do so, we will go deeper into the final stages of the case presented in Chapter 4. We will focus on Orkestra as a research organisation and reflect on its change process since 2009, when we made an explicit decision to create an AR environment.

We understand an AR environment to be a context providing the conditions for researchers to connect action, research and participation. The key to working as an action researcher is not being involved in action, participation and research simultaneously, but rather connecting action, research and participation. We will begin by discussing our approach to action, which will be the first thread in the chapter. We will present the pragmatic approach to action and argue that action is interaction. We will then focus on collective action as a concept that helps to relate action to territorial development. In the case discussion, we will argue that the concept of collective action is insufficient to explain our understanding of territorial development processes, and will propose the concept of aligned action, which is not an alternative concept, but a complement to collective action.

The second thread in the chapter pertains to participation. In discussing this concept, we will first create a framework for understanding how researchers influence their environments. Later, a reflection on practice will lead us to define our research role as political.

Finally, we will pursue a third thread, which is linked to research. We will begin by discussing who is an action researcher, and will then propose, based on our own experience, a pluralistic approach to action research environments.

The term 'pluralistic' can be used to denote that there are different action research approaches, as well as to confront academic research and action research (Svensson and Nielsen, 2006). However, we prefer an approach where pluralism is understood as a respect for other theoretical approaches and their interpretation of a phenomenon – as a certain attitude:[1]

> a kind of humility, admitting that deferring one's own judgement for the benefit of further information and deliberation is preferable when dealing with theoretical issues … a bit more sophisticated version of pluralism implies that one is aware that any particular theory, perspective or approach may be understood differently from how one understands it oneself. This goes along with the recognition that there may be more than one 'relevant' interpretation of the same phenomenon.
> (Pålshaugen, 2013, p. 289)

The Cornerstones of Action Research

ACTION UNDERSTOOD AS INTERACTION

When creating an action research environment, we must generate the conditions that enable researchers to connect to action. The question then emerges: what is action for an action researcher?

We understand that action in a context of territorial development is interaction. Thus, we will discuss individual action versus interaction here. An individual action is a single and individualistic physical movement undertaken with a purpose. It is important in certain fields, such as in ethics and jurisprudence, where we often have to concentrate on one action at a time

---

1   The use of the term 'pluralistic approach' is inspired by a discussion with Øyvind Pålshaugen.

(Kilpinen, 2009). For instance, who threw the stone that broke the window? For the police, this question is crucial.

The pragmatist's notion of action is not the same as the individual action. For a pragmatist, action is human social behaviour as a continuous process. Instead of depicting human activity as a sequence of separate and instantaneous 'actions', pragmatism understands action to be a unified and ongoing process. The acting subject's intentionality and rationality are to be found inside rather than outside that process (Kilpinen, 2003, p. 291). In a social context, action is therefore interaction. We respond to one another's actions so that single actions become interactions – that is, a chain of interwoven actions. In meeting with others, we interact. We act simply by being present in a meeting; we act through talking, by making decisions and by following up on decisions or not following up on them. We believe that interaction between actors is the foundation for creating new knowledge.

The pragmatist's understanding of action creates a bridge over the dualism between mind and body. Action has priority over ideas and principles because the mind and body work together when acting (Reason and Bradbury, 2001). It is not possible to separate thought from action. Ideas, theories and plans can only be judged in terms of their usefulness, workability and practicality. When we act, we are using all of our capabilities and capacity in the action. All types of behaviour become action, including thinking, talking and body language, among others. Thinking is guidance for action. Thinking is a means of reflecting on how a situation can be modified and improved. Connecting with others in conversation is part of the reflection process that leads to change. An idea or a theory is a plan for change; it is an instrument for action (Martinsen, 2011).

However, we must not confuse thought or reflection with discourse. In daily life, we typically assume a connection between talk, decisions and actions – that is, consistent behaviour, so that what can be said can be done, and what can be done can be said. There may be a strong connection between talk and implementation in some cases, but no connection whatsoever in others. Actors, such as politicians or the leaders of an organisation, may talk about doing one thing and then do something else instead. This observation inspired Brunsson (2007) to create the concept of *organised hypocrisy*: 'People may talk or decide about a certain action but act in the opposite way. The result is hypocrisy' (Brunsson, 2007, p. 112). Hypocrisy has negative connotations, and may even be viewed as challenging moral norms. In an organisation that is not executing a decision, this gap is usually deemed an implementation problem.

But Brunsson (2007) argues that hypocrisy is a mechanism for handling conflict between what is said and what can be done. In situations involving conflicting aims or multiple pressures on actors, hypocrisy may be the only solution. It may actually be rational for an organisation to discuss making one type of decision and then do something different or nothing at all.

Action research relates to real-time processes, and hypocrisy is one element that researchers must address and be aware of. The ambiguity between talk and action reflects the reality of processes. Observed in a detached way, hypocrisy may be interpreted as foolish and irrational; however, viewed from the inside out, it can be understood as a rational means to maintain a process.

We now introduce the concept of *collective action*, which will be used in the discussion. Collective action is concerned with the provision of public goods. Territorial development is related to the dilemma of collective benefits, which can be formulated as follows: 'unless the number of individuals is quite small, or unless there is coercion or some other special device to make individuals act in their common interest, rational self-interested individuals will not act to achieve their common or group interests' (Olson, 1965, p. 2). The fact that some individuals do act to achieve common interests and others do not led Ostrom (1990) to study the differences between these individuals. The differences may relate to factors internal to a group:

> *The participants may simply have no capacity to communicate with one another, no way to develop trust, and no sense that they must share a common future. Alternatively, powerful individuals who stand to gain from the current situations, while others lose, may block efforts by the less powerful to change the rules of the game. Such groups may need some form of external assistance to break out [of] the perverse logic of their situation.*
>
> (Ostrom, 1990, p. 21)

This external assistance is one of the roles we see for AR in territorial development. Ostrom goes on to argue that the differences might also relate to factors outside the domain of those affected. Some participants do not have the autonomy to change their own institutional structures and are prevented from making constructive changes by external authorities. As long as analysts presume that individuals cannot change such situations themselves, they do not ask what internal or external variables can enhance or impede the efforts of communities to address their problems creatively and constructively

(Ostrom, 1990, p. 21). Becoming aware of how such internal and external variables affect action and understanding that this awareness is part of action itself is at the core of our approach to action research for territorial development.

PARTICIPATION

Researchers in the social sciences have long debated the influence of the researcher on the object of study. In Chapter 1 we reflected on the presence of researchers in territorial development processes as one more type of actor. But this position is often considered artificial, and some researchers try to determine what would have happened if the researcher had not been present and events had followed their 'natural' course. This is, of course, a valid attempt, though a methodological challenge for those researchers who want to maintain distance from the topic being studied. However, we believe that the distinction between the researcher and the object of study is less clear than is often assumed, even within the natural sciences. In a classical laboratory experiment, the researcher can control one variable at a time while keeping the other variables constant. By repeating the experiments several times and changing one variable at a time, the connection between cause and effect can be detected and measured. However, even within the natural sciences, such as in the case of quantum mechanics in physics, particles smaller than atoms are influenced by measurements (Ledford and Susan, 1993). Thus, it is difficult to find situations where the researcher avoids exerting an influence on the outcome.

This is a challenge researchers in all fields encounter when attempting to connect with actors in a process. In social processes, influence cannot be avoided (Bjørndal, 2004; Hammersley, 1995). We may influence a process by participating in it, or even by being physically present without saying a word. Influence can be verbal or non-verbal. It may exert its effects in a formal meeting or during an informal conversation after a meeting. Researchers may influence a change process by talking to people, by asking questions or giving suggestions, or by giving a speech and telling stories from other processes, as researchers often do. Influence can occur in open dialogues or in closed agoras with a few powerful actors. It can be formal or informal, and fast or slow. There may be a difference between what is presented formally in official documents and presentations and what is said during a meeting or done after a meeting. All of these elements may influence the process.

The AR approach seeks to understand how change processes occur through all of these types of interactions. In many research processes where there is no such awareness, influence is measured in terms of the impact of publications and formal presentations. When attempting to establish an AR environment, conditions should be created not only for these formal and often one-directional processes to occur and be measured, but also for the informal and interactive processes to develop. For a pragmatist, this approach is critical because participation is behaviour – continuous action.

In this respect, there is a difference between the anthropologist and the action researcher. The former wants to influence the situation as little as possible. The latter is focused on how to alter a situation and contribute to solving a problem. The action researcher must be aware that he or she influences the other participants and the situation. Often, researchers who participate in change processes are not aware of their influence.

There is a difference between a research process that is performed completely by researchers (in which the researchers control the process even if they interact with territorial actors to obtain data) and a participatory process (where the researcher can influence a process, but not control it). In fact, the researcher has no right to control the process. Action research is a participatory process, and AR environments should create favourable conditions for researchers to influence and be influenced by the process in a conscious manner. Participating in situations of territorial complexity and trying to generate an actionable solution is not easy. It can be frustrating. However, when a researcher is invited to participate in a process – to solve a problem – with other actors, it is neither possible nor desirable for him or her to control the process. The challenge for the researcher is how to be one more participant in the process that influences the situation, with as much awareness as possible of how each participant contributes to change.

RESEARCH

Together with action and participation, research is a cornerstone of action research. In the process of generating an AR environment, it is possible to create an agora that supports researchers' connection to action and participation. However, if researchers do not commit to working in this way, no action research environment can exist.

Action researchers become involved in change processes. Does this statement imply that all researchers who participate in change processes are action researchers? Our initial answer was, in principle, yes. At the end of this section, we will explain why this is not our final answer; but first, let us share our reflection process.

Not all researchers who participate in change processes consider themselves to be action researchers. Some researchers are not interested in this discussion at all. Other researchers within the social sciences are interested in studying change processes, but do not participate in them. Some might say that researchers should not be participating in change processes at all, whereas others might say that it is the aim of research to contribute to change based on knowledge. A variety of positions exist regarding researchers' participation in change processes.

Referring to those researchers who claim to be action researchers, Pålshaugen (2007) argues that action research is not really part of the social research establishment, nor is there really something like an 'action research establishment'. Today, he says, action research is indeed widespread, but that means widely spread. He argues that it is the combination of a weak institutional basis and a strong personal engagement that often leads many action researchers to identify themselves rather personally with their role as action researcher. He argues that this approach does not hold water due to the diversity within action research and the lack of one unique perspective on what action research is. While we agree with the weak institutional basis for action research, we still believe that the explicit identification of researchers as action researchers is a relevant element when creating action research environments.

To help us reflect on this issue, we created several four-field tables. We share one of them in Table 5.1. The first dimension in the table is whether researchers participate in change processes. By using the words *researcher, participate* and *change process*, we aim to reflect on the cornerstones of AR: research, participation and action. Participation must entail direct interaction between territorial actors and researchers rather than participation from a distance or on paper (Gustavsen, 1992). But would a researcher involved in action and participation still be an action researcher if he or she did not claim to be one? There is a subjective element in the positioning of someone as an action researcher. Consequently, the second dimension is whether the researcher considers him- or herself to be an action researcher. The answer is not as simple as might first appear; it is founded upon the researcher's definition of research and his or her perspective on how new knowledge can be generated in a sound and valid manner.[2] The combination

---

2   In the concluding reflections we will return to the issue of validity when summing up the main discussions in the book.

of the two dimensions yields four different types of research position. The first position is that of the *declared action researcher*, who participates in change processes and presents him- or herself as an action researcher. The second position is that of the *theoretical action researcher*. This type considers him- or herself part of the community of action research, but does not directly participate in change processes. Although this position might appear to be contradictory, the researcher believes in the cornerstones of action research and may be more interested in the philosophy and theory of science than in participation. In our experience, this researcher has often been an active participant in prior participatory processes, and often acts as an adviser for researchers participating in change processes. In the fourth position, we find researchers who do not participate in change processes and who do not consider themselves to be action researchers.

Our dilemmas primarily emerged when discussing researchers of type III. If a researcher works with change processes but does not consider him- or herself to be an action researcher, what type of researcher is he or she? It may be that he or she feels that 'action researcher' is not a good descriptive title. Some do not like the label 'action research'. Many of those in this group are discipline-oriented researchers who lend their knowledge to research on change processes in the hope of benefiting society.

We understand that a researcher's self-identification as an action researcher is important because accompanying it is the recognition of certain principles for research. It brings connection to a community of action researchers who make a specific type of contribution to the academic world. It also brings exposure to the criticism and scepticism AR faces in the academic community. For this reason, a researcher's placement in the 'undeclared action researcher' category may sometimes reflect a lack of awareness of the existence of AR as a community and a body of literature. It may also reflect a conscious decision on the part of the researcher.

Table 5.1   Types of researchers

| | | Participate in change processes in the territory? | |
		Yes	No
Consider themselves to be action researchers?	Yes	I. Declared action researcher	II. Theoretical action researcher
	No	III. Undeclared action researcher	IV. Not an action researcher

But is an association with action and participation sufficient to consider oneself an action researcher? With the approach to participation we have presented, in which it is impossible to avoid influencing a subject, would not all researchers be considered action researchers? Our answer is no. Thus, we missed something crucial in the first approach.

The action researcher must contribute to the academic community using his or her experience from participating in change processes. It is not enough to say that one is an action researcher and that one participates in change processes; one must also reflect these processes back to the academic community. Many disciplinary researchers act as consultants in addition to their university work. They reflect on practice, but their writing is often disconnected from their experience, or not connected to it in an explicit way. Their experience-based knowledge remains tacit because they do not view this type of knowledge as valuable for the scientific community. For the disciplinary researcher, this is not necessarily a problem. For an action researcher, however, it should be. Action researchers must be aware of the need to contribute to academia from experience.

Consequently, our interpretation of the three cornerstones of action research supplied by Greenwood and Levin (2007) is that an action researcher is not only involved in research, action and participation, he or she must pursue these activities in a connected way. For example, a researcher may participate in change processes and publish in academic journals. The question is whether the writing is based on his or her experience of participation and action, or is that of an outside observer.

If we return to Table 5.1 and substitute the subjective positioning criterion with the criterion of whether a researcher contributes to academia based on his or her experience, the discussion would revolve around two types of researchers who participate in change processes. The first group of researchers do not connect their experience to the academic debate, which does not imply that they are not contributing to the academic community. The second group of researchers are writing from the inside out, connecting their knowledge from experience to the academy. We want to encourage researchers that have experience in territorial development, but are not writing based on it, to do so.

A fine line or a broad chasm may separate researchers with different profiles in a research environment. The interrelations across this separation may be essential in creating a space for action research in the academic community. None of the classifications we have used in this section would make sense if they were not now used to reflect on how researchers with different approaches relate to each other in the context of AR environments. That critical thread weaves through this chapter's case study discussion in the following sections.

Case: Orkestra, Part 2

ACTION RESEARCH: ENTERING THE DEBATE WITH OTHER APPROACHES

As we stated in the introduction to this chapter, in 2009 a decision was made to support the creation of an action research environment in Orkestra. As one of the first steps, a delegation from the Basque Country, composed of researchers from Orkestra and policy makers from the Basque Government, asked to visit Agderforskning in Norway to learn about how Norwegian researchers engaged in AR. Both authors of this book were at that meeting, Miren Larrea as part of the Basque delegation, James Karlsen as part of the Norwegian one. The Norwegian researchers proposed that the Basque representatives should read Greenwood and Levin (2007) and reflect on the institute's situation. Only then should the visit be undertaken.

This initial reading was not neutral. If we had chosen a different book to guide our first reflections on Orkestra as an AR environment, our environment would probably have developed in a different way. The choice was influenced by one of us being trained as action researcher in the pragmatic approach, and it was the beginning of the influence of pragmatism on the way the Orkestra group approached AR. We used the reflections on Greenwood and Levin's book to write a report on what was needed to create an AR environment. The report was circulated among the Norwegian researchers participating in the meeting, but it was not circulated within Orkestra. In retrospect, we were afraid that our document would be interpreted as a suggestion that there were two ways to approach research, and that only one was useful in generating change. It was written in terms of a dichotomy between traditional research and AR.

Together with this, Greenwood and Levin's (2007) discussion of action research versus traditional research had made us feel relieved. For some years, we had experienced a growing pressure about our 'non-scientific' approach to research, but finally we had found a path to release this pressure. Our document was written as a kind of self-defence argument to those criticising our previous research, but we were aware that it could be understood as an attack on 'traditional research'. We were interpreting an action research environment to be a context for action researchers, and we felt isolated in that position inside our own organisation.

The feeling we had about the document materialised in the daily life of the institute. The proposal to develop AR in Orkestra was received positively by some and with discomfort by others. It generated a kind of schism at the institute. At the time of writing this book, discussing this chapter with Orkestra researchers who were there at that time, we have confirmed this. Still, one of the reflections was that it was probably necessary to create this tension in order to generate the perception of AR as a distinct approach that was different to what we were already doing. Had the process been softer and not generated such discomfort, AR might never have developed in the institute. We have chosen two discussions to illustrate how the situation evolved from this initial schism. One is the discussion about the approach to AR, the second has to do with the spaces and work groups created in Orkestra to work on AR.

After the visit to Agder, we continued to reflect on our approach to research in Orkestra and action research. In a type of mirror effect with what we had named 'the Norwegian way to AR', the description 'the Basque way to AR' emerged in the dialogue. In a seminar about AR, a British researcher criticised the use of these terms. He argued that it was restrictive for researchers to include themselves in a school of thought that framed their research. Discussion of this argument led to another term, 'the Orkestra way to AR', suggesting that we did not need a school of thought but should share some perspectives among the members of our team. Eventually, this term faded too. When constructing this chapter, one of the Orkestra researchers claimed that there is an Orkestra way to AR. But the term was no longer part of the discourse.

The second discussion, which ran parallel to the previous process, illustrates what we think is the same trend. Shortly after the visit to Agderforskning, a group of researchers interested in learning about AR was created within Orkestra. We met every month to discuss different issues related to AR and to create common ground. The evolution of the group was reflected in its changing names. Initially, it was called 'the Core Group for AR'. In one of the group's meetings, concern arose that this name might create confrontation between AR and other research approaches at the institute. Only a few of the group's members wanted AR to be the main focus of their research. We decided that the group itself would not have a name, and that the meetings would be called 'action research meetings'. Although there was no explicit reflection in the group about it, the group slowly disintegrated. Those researchers interested in AR found their own approach to AR. When the co-ordinator of one of the areas asked what to do about this group disintegrating, we realised that AR was developing in specific projects and that there should be a focus on projects rather than on a specific group of action researchers. Action research had diffused throughout the institute, generating reflective processes as part of different projects, but without a distinct group of action researchers within the organisation. In many of the projects, action research was combined with other approaches. Most of all, researchers began to combine action research knowledge with specific expert knowledge, leading to the definition of mixed concepts such as 'engaged governance' (Karlsen, 2010) or 'action research for territorial development', which we discuss in this book. The line between action research and 'traditional research' blurred. The teams were no longer AR teams. Still, AR was accepted and present to a greater degree than before in some of Orkestra's critical projects.

CONSTRUCTING THE NEW APPROACH

While the debates presented in the previous section were taking place and making the most noise, the approach to AR in Orkestra was silently shaped in specific research processes. One of the main elements taken from the pragmatic approach was Greenwood and Levin's (2007) cogenerative AR model presented in Chapter 4. It helped us to reflect on how projects had developed in previous years. When using this model, we realised that a group of researchers was already developing processes that fitted the model quite easily. Different types of agoras had been established, trust relationships with actors were developing, and there were examples of action deriving from reflective processes. One project was linked to a previous project, so the cyclical perspective of the model was also detected in practice. The feeling began to emerge that action research had been under way for some time, although the term had not been used. Consequently, some researchers began to construct a discourse of AR that they used in their interactions with practitioners.

Frustrations and new expectations developed in the process. At the beginning, explicit instructions were expected from the Norwegian partners on how to create an AR environment. Instead, mostly new questions were delivered. This dynamic created a certain level of puzzlement at the beginning. Later, it facilitated reflection. Proposals were made about regularly holding debriefing sessions after the meetings with actors and keeping diaries.[3] Debriefing sessions were held fairly regularly, but diary-keeping seemed too difficult to make a habit. Still, as a consequence of apparently small changes, a new style of writing about AR processes emerged (see Karlsen et al., 2012; Karlsen and Larrea, 2012; Aranguren and Larrea, 2011; Estensoro and Larrea, 2012).[4] Our learning on AR was not only affecting how we interacted with actors, but also how we interacted with the academic community.

Case Discussion: Constructing the Connections for Action Research

We now present the results of our reflections on the process. We have already shared our main reflection: creating an AR environment is not only about generating the three cornerstones of AR, but also about connecting them. Researchers at Orkestra were already involved in action, in research and in interaction, but the discussions on AR led some of the researchers to consciously connect the three. Pragmatism's primary contribution was not the establishment of any one of the cornerstones, but their connection. Thus, the first discussions in this section pertain to the connection between research and action on the one hand and research and participation on the other. The final discussion relates to another connection that appears as a thread throughout the case study: the connection between disciplinary research and action research.

CONNECTING RESEARCH TO ACTION

The first time researchers from Orkestra travelled to Agder, we were accompanied by policy makers from the Basque Country. There was a feeling from the beginning that AR was not about only the researchers changing, but about practitioners and researchers changing together. This realisation was critical in initiating the action research approach.

The trip to Agder took place in February 2009, and in May 2009 a workshop was held with the main practitioners in territorial development networks in the Basque Country. The participants in the Agder study trip, together with one of the researchers from Norway, presented the concept of AR to the participants. The policy makers also played an active role in the presentations. That day,

---

3   In these sessions, every member of the research team discussed the answers to four questions: What happened? How did I feel? How do I think others felt? What should we change for next time?

4   As described in the later discussion, previously there was an understanding of data as very much based on structured databases with either quantitative or qualitative data.

the decision was made to create the Action Network, which would develop action research processes among researchers and practitioners representing co-operation networks for economic territorial development in the region (coming from local development agencies, cluster associations and regional networks for innovation and competitiveness related to provincial councils and the Basque Government).

When practitioners and researchers in the Action Network met to learn how to improve networking processes, the learning process was in itself an action, understood from the pragmatic perspective as interaction. However, this learning was not the end goal in itself; rather, practitioners aimed to learn in order to later change or improve their networks. In some cases, practitioners reported back about the changes they had made due to their interactions with researchers. In other cases, they did not. Sometimes, practitioners were probably unaware that the reflection process with researchers had influenced their behaviour. Others expressed such influence explicitly, but it was difficult to separate it from the myriad of factors affecting their networks. Still, though they were not always recognised and were always difficult to measure, the change processes practitioners launched after the AR workshops were essential to our approach. The last meeting of the Action Network was held in 2011, but we continued working on AR terms with many of the participants in the process.

We will now share our perspective on the interaction between research and action inspired by this process. The relationships developed in this process were loose and did not respond to a closed plan. Despite that, we do not consider the changes participants made in their networks as unintended consequences of the research process. The changes may have been unpredictable or unplanned, but they were not unintended. The entire process was oriented towards creating the conditions for those changes to happen, without a specific plan for exactly what would happen and how.

The creation of the Action Network and the learning processes are actions. In this case, we refer to them as *collective actions*. But there was a second wave of action that transcended the collective action. It was the result of the practitioners undertaking change processes, this time in their own networks. This time there was no direct participation by researchers, but change was influenced by knowledge cogenerated in the AR process. We called this wave *aligned action*. Aligned action is action undertaken by practitioners who are autonomous but share frameworks that influence their decisions. The influence of the shared frameworks on each action might be imperceptible. But all small actions inspired by the shared frameworks generate a trend in a specific direction. Aligned action in a territory – if sustained over time – can create the conditions for macro change. Aligned action is one of the features of many of the AR processes developed in Orkestra.

A NEW UNDERSTANDING OF WRITING FROM EXPERIENCE

One of the steps for consolidating the connection between research and action in Orkestra was the learning process on how to write from experience. We find this part of the AR process more important than is often suggested in the AR literature, as it is in the writing process where one of the critical connections between research, action and participation occurs.

Because of our training and the expectations that prevail in our academic field, we separated thought from action before reflecting on the principles of AR. We participated in processes with practitioners and became engaged in and committed to the output of the process. However, when the time came to reflect and write, we wrote as we had been trained to, not considering our own experience as data. In terms of the pragmatic approach presented earlier, we were separating thought in the writing process from action.

In the interviews with Orkestra researchers to check the validity of this chapter, one argued that at that time there was an understanding of quantitative analysis as the basis for rigorous research, and a concern that a shift towards AR could mean unbalancing the research at the institute towards more qualitative, and thus less rigorous, research. Consequently, one of the critical steps in the development of AR was overcoming this perception and being able to publish in journals that would be recognised by peers.

We had worked on the principle that data were mainly quantitative indicators given by statistical institutes or either quantitative or qualitative data gathered though questionnaires. We had not been trained to use practitioners' statements and our discussions with them as data. We had not used the minutes and reports from meetings. A contradiction in our approach became clear. We had been developing processes related to Greenwood and Levin's (2007) cogenerative model. However, we had been writing as if we were involved in a project with statistical data or surveys as the main source of data. Our data were very weak in that respect, as they were the by-product of a process that had not been designed to obtain them. However, when interpreting the data, we clearly had knowledge about the process that was not directly derived from it. It should be no surprise that a reviewer from an international journal responded that he or she had the feeling that 'there were two stories going on in the article and maybe it would be wiser to write two'. That was the moment when we decided to be explicit about AR in our academic output.

As we argued above, writing from the researcher's experience in change processes is not an extended approach in RIS and territorial development. AR generates tacit knowing – researchers know more than they can describe with words. Consequently, the key to writing from experience is to try to make tacit knowing explicit. AR data are less structured than those gleaned from statistics or surveys. It is difficult to see what the main lessons learnt are and to find a writing style that fits with our own approach to research. Nevertheless, it is important to do so. The process of writing from experience can be exhausting. But failing to try to make tacit knowing explicit may hinder the learning process of the action researcher and the consolidation of AR in specific environments.

Territorial development based on RISs faces the challenge of creating contexts in which action researchers and their knowledge are integrated with the rest of the field. There is a type of understanding of change processes that can only be obtained from within a process. The knowledge an action researcher can generate about how and why change happens cannot be obtained using other methodologies. In the example discussed, we obtained relevant knowledge from processes, but we were writing about the field as though we were analysing it from the outside. One of the main arguments in this book is that the academic community can obtain vital insights regarding change processes by supporting researchers who write from their own experience in the field.

CONNECTING RESEARCH TO PARTICIPATION

Through our first contact with action research, the researchers in Orkestra learnt about tools for dialogue and learning, such as search conferences and dialogue conferences that could be used to construct the agora. These were carefully designed events where researchers and practitioners interacted in search of a solution to the problem they were facing. Although we did not use these terms and there were various differences from what they described, we were already using similar processes by developing workshops with the territorial actors, mainly local development agencies. Eventually, however, we became aware that another approach to participation was developing.

This approach was perhaps more risky and problematic because practitioners were less aware that research was taking place. Yet it could be at least as influential as the previous approach. We were invited to participate in policy reflection and design processes with policy makers, and thereby became integrated into some of their boards and committees. This participation was defined as a research process, and the roles were made clear every time a project began. However, practitioners viewed this participation as part of their routines, and it was not always easy to visualise our contribution to the process as research. We were not to become one more policy maker in the policy making teams. From this position, we could generate deeper learning processes on their routines than we could through workshops. But the issue of critical distance and the discussions regarding the roles of insiders and outsiders became crucial for the definition and development of participation. We were aware that we were becoming involved in processes that were essential to generate change in the territory. But we were also becoming involved with powerful interests, and it was not always easy to determine whether we were playing a role we should.

Besides the challenge of not becoming one more practitioner in the process, this dilemma also prompted discussions regarding issues such as the difference between research and consultancy (Aranguren et al., 2012b). Facilitating a process was perceived by some as being the role of consultants, not researchers. This argument was mostly used by other researchers, and to a lesser extent by practitioners.

All these discussions led to a growing awareness that simply by being present, a researcher influences a process. We have noted that this is a problem for some researchers, but we suggest that it is not a problem for an action researcher who aims to change a situation through research. However it is essential to be aware of how such influence takes place. In our case, the reflection process on AR made us aware that we were entering processes with our own concrete understanding of the desired change in terms of territorial development. This is something researchers do not usually make explicit. As a result, we were political actors in the territory, with our own agendas for change. This recalls the discussion in Chapter 4 regarding the role of research organisations in particular territories. Orkestra was created with the aim of fomenting *real* competitiveness in the Basque Country. The goal was not only to understand competitiveness, but also to generate it. Researchers analysing and interacting with territorial actors develop their own views on the changes that are desirable. A researcher who interacts with practitioners influences them even when he or she remains silent. This influence responds to certain values, principles and interpretations of the situation. It is impossible to relinquish these personal influences and seek instead the neutrality that some research approaches argue for. The initiation of a project is always a process of negotiation wherein the researcher must make his or her position clear and only enter the process if his or her values, principles and interpretation of the situation are compatible with practitioners'. The perspectives of researchers and practitioners do not necessarily need to be coincident; there would be no opportunity to learn and change if this was so. However, practitioners must be aware of researchers' agenda for change. To avoid manipulation by either party, it is important that this discussion continues throughout the process.

In this context, where researchers are political actors, what are the main contributions of AR and the creation of an AR environment? In Orkestra, AR was an instrument for empowering researchers who entered processes with practitioners (primarily policy makers). The AR approach provided us with a discourse shared by a research community. AR gave us consistent arguments regarding the need to maintain a critical distance. We used these arguments when entering complicated discussions involving strong power dynamics. AR provided a connection to research environments around the world that contributed knowledge and supported our position when negotiating our role with policy makers. It gave us a more solid position not only in relation to the academic community, but also in our interactions with policy makers.

While writing this book, we found this discussion of the researcher as political actor in the territory to be one of the most intricate we were facing. That is why we will develop it further in Chapter 7 with a discussion on neutrality based on the contribution of Paulo Freire.

Taking the Discussion Further: A Pluralistic Approach to AR

The case study depicts a process that began with a dichotomised approach to action research and ended in a pluralistic approach whereby action research is connected to other research approaches, teams are mixed and AR develops in relation to other disciplinary fields, mainly territorial development and policy learning. There is an environment for AR in Orkestra, but it is so mixed with other research approaches and other disciplinary fields that it would be difficult to isolate.

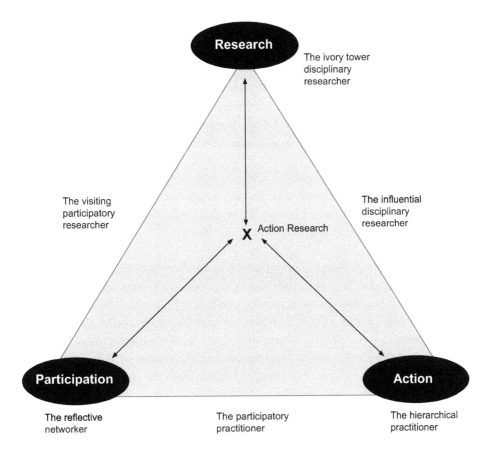

Figure 5.1   The action research triangle

The following discussion of how and why a pluralistic approach developed will help us to reflect on how AR adapts to specific environments and how creating the right conditions to connect action, participation and research results from a learning process that evolves differently in each situation. We could say that the approach to AR in Orkestra evolved so that the AR approach could survive and be accepted by the local research community, but also because it required the knowledge generated in other disciplinary fields. AR became consolidated through a team approach – not a team of action researchers, but rather heterogeneous teams of researchers and practitioners.

In the case study, we mentioned a group of researchers who met regularly to discuss action research. This group included 11 researchers, all but one of whom considered themselves to be participating in change processes in the region.

At least five had published internationally from their experiences, but only three considered themselves to be action researchers. Thus, action research was developing in an environment populated by both action researchers and non-action researchers. To depict the heterogeneity of profiles participating in processes in Orkestra, we have arranged the different roles in the shape of a triangle (see Figure 5.1). Our first attempt placed only researchers in the triangle; then we realised that practitioners should also be represented as part of AR teams.

The *ivory tower disciplinary researchers* relate exclusively to the research community. They influence territory through other researchers who take their work and integrate it in processes with practitioners.

The *influential disciplinary researchers* also create knowledge in the disciplinary academic community, in interaction with other researchers and without being involved in participatory processes. However, these researchers are in contact with practitioners when transferring their knowledge and can be recognised by the practice community that reads or listens to them. These researchers' knowledge can be transferred in a linear manner through reports, academic publications and conferences, or can be used by other researchers involved in participatory processes.

The *visiting participatory researchers* can be engaged in a long-term process in the territory, but only interact sporadically with territorial actors, so cannot be in charge of facilitating the long-term process. They can facilitate specific workshops or meetings and share expert knowledge with practitioners. They connect to practitioners in a specific moment, then exit the location.

The *reflective networkers* are responsible for organising arenas for shared reflection among actors. When these practitioners are located in the extreme corner of the triangle, it means that they are facilitating participation that is not connected to action or to research. This means that there are no mechanisms in the participatory process to integrate new concepts and frameworks from research or mechanisms to take the results of such reflection into action.

The *participatory practitioners* develop participatory processes and connect them to action, but when positioned in the lowest part of the triangle, do not integrate concepts and frameworks from research nor reflect on practice to make a contribution to research.

The *hierarchical practitioners* are responsible for action, but are empowered to make decisions without the influence of other actors or research.

All of the roles situated on the outer edges of the triangle are extreme positions or caricatures. Most researchers and practitioners are located somewhere inside the triangle, in more mixed positions. We have positioned action research in the middle of the triangle in a perfect balance between research, action and participation. This balance is difficult, although not impossible, to achieve. But the position does not represent a single researcher or practitioner. It rather represents the balance for which a multidisciplinary team should strive. Each member of the team contributes a unique perspective to this balance.

The ability to be an action researcher is not only related to the ability to position oneself in the centre of the triangle. It also relates to the ability to position the results of research developed by teams composed of researchers and practitioners with diverse experience and interests as close to the centre of the triangle as possible. Thus, we conclude that AR concerns both individual and collective capabilities. We checked the validity of this framework with researchers in Orkestra. One of them, who had to a great extent inspired the figure of the influential disciplinary researcher, was faced with the question of whether an extreme interpretation of the framework would mean that there can be an action research environment without action researchers. Although he agreed that action research had integrated a variety of researchers positioned all over the triangle, he underlined the relevance of having a small group close to the centre to make it all possible. We agree with this. The creation of a pluralistic approach to AR was not a spontaneous process in Orkestra. It needed a firm decision from a few to position themselves as close to the centre as they could. This made it possible to generate the conditions to create an environment for AR that opened far beyond such a central position. So even though the process was pushed by action researchers, generating an action research environment was not a matter of creating a group of action researchers. Instead, this process involved generating the conditions for researchers with different profiles and actors who wanted to work together to do so. We are not certain whether we have created an AR environment, but we have created an environment for AR. It is a pluralistic environment in which AR and disciplinary research in the field complement and reinforce one another.

Closing Comments

We understand the term 'pluralistic action research environment' to refer to a research environment that connects the three elements of participation, action and research, and where there are many different theoretical contributions to knowledge cogeneration.

We believe there is a great opportunity for growth in action research for territorial development at the intersection of action research and disciplinary approaches to territorial development. The way forward is the creation of agoras so that researchers with different backgrounds can connect, interact and cogenerate new knowledge together with other actors in the territory.

We know it is not necessarily easy to be a declared action researcher in the field of territorial development. But we also believe that action research with pluralistic approaches can catalyse change processes with very few declared action researchers. To achieve this, they must get involved with researchers with other profiles in territorial development disciplines. That is why, although AR approaches can be criticised by some in the territorial development research community, we must avoid the temptation of using AR environments as trenches where we hide from such criticism. Pluralistic AR environments are environments where there may be disciplinary researchers with very critical opinions about AR who not only coexist, but can work together with action researchers in change processes.

This is not something an individual researcher can do alone. In the previous chapters we have argued for the role of social researchers as agents of change in territorial development processes. But to do so, certain conditions need to be created, and they do not only refer to individual researchers that approach the field. They have to do with the goals of research organisations, how they integrate different approaches to research and how researchers configure teams to approach the field.

As with any other strategy for territorial development, the creation of an AR environment changes greatly from the design on paper to the actual implementation. AR does not develop in a vacuum, and it needs to find its place among other approaches. This chapter has discussed this process from the inside out. It is not a matter of the rationally optimising solution. Again, it is a story of researchers of flesh, bones and feelings. It is a story of mutual recognition among researchers with different perspectives. The terms and concepts used have evolved to facilitate this. These are the reasons why there are no recipes for how to create action research environments for territorial development. Every combination of researchers, motivations, interests, power play and organisational culture is different. Every environment for action research and territorial development is unique. Nevertheless, we hope our self-reflective process can inspire others who wish to develop such environments.

Finally, action research environments must be resilient, adaptive and reflective so that they can be as aware of their own transformation as possible. In this sense, the case study depicted a trajectory towards a pluralistic approach. In other cases, the transformation may move in different directions. In all of them, self-reflection by research teams may provide interesting insights for others who are making similar efforts.

PART III
Innovation through Dialogue

In Part III we will argue that dialogue is the main process in the agora. We have often experienced that language as a medium for communication is inaccurate and full of ambiguities. We mean to say one thing, but this may be interpreted in a quite different way, which can create challenges for territorial development processes as well as for daily communication.

Linguistic researchers such as Noam Chomsky (1966; 2010) have explained this is a result of an evolutionary process where language was first developed as a tool for self-reflection, and that language as a tool for communication was an accidental effect of this biological process. According to Chomsky, this explains why language as a medium for communication is inaccurate and ambiguous.

We cannot do anything about the inbuilt ambiguity of language. We have to acknowledge that language is inaccurate for communication, but it is the best tool we have. It is the tool for connection between people, and thus for territorial development and for innovation. Since we cannot control the precision of language, we have to focus on the conditions we can do something about. We have to develop strategies for handling the ambiguousness of language in communication. How language and communication can help to construct dialogue is one of the topics for this part of the book.

In the following chapters we will explore dialogue as a means for change and innovation more deeply. We will examine how two researchers have worked with dialogue as a tool for change in two very different social contexts. One of them is the Norwegian work life researcher Bjørn Gustavsen (Chapter 6), and the other is the Brazilian pedagogue Paulo Freire (Chapter 7). We will argue that dialogue and their burning desire to change society are common factors that unite them despite geographical distance.

6

Dialogue and Development

At the end of 2011 a workshop was held as part of a project on which researchers and policy makers in the Provincial Council of Gipuzkoa (one of the provinces of the Basque Country) had been working together for two years. In a sense it was a kick-off meeting, as the government had changed and this was the first time most of the new elected politicians and researchers had met face to face. There was uncertainty about the continuation of the project. When one of the politicians gave an introduction, he said that he felt it was a historical moment, a moment of change, because they were coming not from being in opposition, but from being out of the political game altogether.[1] Their challenge was to build both political and social bridges. When asked by a researcher to be more concrete about the bridges, he said that what had been happening until then was not only disagreement, but lack of communication. They needed a new language, as the terms that were being used had deteriorated. He then spoke directly to the researchers from abroad and told them that they had an important role to play as they were outsiders to such deteriorated language and could help create a new language.

Language and dialogue are essential for change and are the core of the agoras for territorial development. We think this is an issue that has been under-studied in the territorial development literature. In this chapter we will revisit Gustavsen's (1992) concept of democratic dialogue as a link between reflection and action leading to change. Democratic dialogue can help to avoid situations where there is either just talk or just action. By doing so, it demonstrates the important role of language.

New language is not just words. We will argue that its construction process is tightly linked to status and how this is distributed among researchers and policy makers in the agora. Change in patterns of communication is critical

---

1   Some political parties had been banned in 2003, and they had participated in the 2011 elections as part of a coalition.

to the generation of change in territorial development. There are a myriad of examples in territorial development where new words have been adopted by both researchers and policy makers. Past and present examples include industrial districts, clusters, learning regions, multi-level governance, regional innovation systems, triple helix and SMART (Specific, Measurable, Attainable, Relevant and Time-bound) specialisation. New words are often related to the latest trend or to cases that have been considered best practice. But if we carefully observe what happened, often little changed except the words. Patterns of communication and status remained the same, which meant policy only changed on the surface. However, it is a mistake to interpret the agora as the space where policy makers and researchers just 'talk'. The agora is also a space for change in territorial development, and we will use Gustavsen's contributions to discuss how to avoid agoras becoming a space where only words change.

We will use the case study of Gipuzkoa Sarean, a social capital and competitiveness project later redefined as a territorial development project, to propose an interpretation of Gustavsen's framework adapted to territorial development purposes.

Principles for a Democratic Dialogue

Bjørn Gustavsen's concept of *democratic dialogue* is the main concept in this chapter. Democratic dialogue is about communication between people in the agora and how that communication can become democratic by accepting and using shared principles in the dialogue. Dialogue is talk, but not only talk, as our interest is in how talk is connected to practice and how practice can be changed through communication. As Gustavsen puts it: 'the major advantage of action research compared to the production of "words alone" is the creation of practices' (Gustavsen, 2008, p. 63).

Gustavsen developed the concept of democratic dialogue in his book *Dialogue and Development* (Gustavsen, 1992). The discussion in the book is based on a five-year research project in Sweden called the LOM (Ledning, Organisation och Medbestämmande – Leadership, Organisation and Codetermination) programme.[2] The purpose of the programme was to initiate and support the

---

2   According to Gustavsen, the practice of the concepts used in the LOM programme was developed earlier through the development and implementation of Terms of Enterprise Development in 1982 between the Norwegian Confederation of Trade Unions and the Confederation of Norwegian Enterprise.

development of new forms of work and enterprise organisation, generated by labour and management together, and to develop a role for research within this context. With the concept of democratic dialogue, Gustavsen emphasised the connection between change in dialogue and change in practice. 'Dialogue' is defined as a free and open conversation between equal partners for the purpose of reaching agreement (Gustavsen, 1992). Gustavsen operationalised the concept in terms of 13 principles for democratic dialogue, which he later refined (Gustavsen, 2001b, pp. 18–19):

1.   Dialogue is based on a principle of give and take, not one-way communication.

2.   All concerned by the issue under discussion should have the possibility of participation.

3.   Participants are under an obligation to help other participants to be active in the dialogue.

4.   All participants have the same status in the dialogue arenas.[3]

5.   Work experience is the point of departure for participation.

6.   Some of the experience the participant has when entering the dialogue must be seen as relevant.

7.   It must be possible for all participants to gain an understanding of the topics under discussion.

8.   An argument can be rejected only after an investigation (and not, for instance, on the grounds that it emanates from a source with limited legitimacy).

9.   All arguments that are to enter the dialogue must be represented by actors present.

10. All participants are obliged to accept that other participants may have arguments better than their own.

---

3   Gustavsen (2001b) uses the term 'rank' instead of 'status'.

11.   Among the issues that can be made subject to discussion are the ordinary work roles of the participants – no one is exempt from such a discussion.

12.   The dialogue should be able to integrate a growing degree of disagreement.

13.   The dialogue should continuously generate decisions that provide a platform for joint action.

Gustavsen emphasises that these criteria are meant to be a preliminary operationalisation, not a final list. However, as time has passed, the criteria have become known as Gustavsen's 13 Principles for Democratic Dialogue. They are ideal principles and procedures for *how* to participate in a dialogue, and *who* can participate in it. They are not principles that make it possible to interpret the intentions of the participants in the dialogue or to help separate a good argument from a bad one (Johnsen, 2001).

Gustavsen's theoretical foundation is participative democracy. He argues strongly in favour of participation by the many instead of by just a handful of actors. His idea of democracy is inspired by the American pragmatist John Dewey's approach to democracy. Gustavsen's argument is that democracy is about social development. It is freedom for self-development, learning and development of skills for interaction and collaboration. From this point of view, it is the participation of many actors in the process that creates legitimacy for a solution, not discussion among a few about the content of a solution. It is the totality the participants bring to the table that is important to discuss, not a single problem defined as relevant by a few. For a person who wants order, control, system and logic, this might sound chaotic, unstructured and loose. But his point is to gather a loose set of people, topics and ideas for discussion that will lead to action. The process is ongoing, minimally structured and stepwise. Gustavsen argues that it is unrealistic to try to create 'big jumps' in solutions – to launch solutions that can create changes overnight. Today's situation is a result of long term ongoing processes that cannot be solved in the short term. A change process is evolutionary, slow and incremental.

The aim of a democratic dialogue is to generate decisions that provide a platform for joint action. The method Gustavsen proposes is the *dialogue conference*, in which researchers and practitioners meet in a carefully designed context based on the 13 principles.[4] Gustavsen (2001b, p. 22) reflects on the interpretation of joint action. He argues that it is often assumed that the main purpose of a discourse is to get the participants to 'look in the same way' at something – for example, a situation, an understanding, a plan of action. He calls conferences with this aim 'single-product events', but also describes 'relationship-building events'. The argument is that in the same way that it is meaningful to have a common story, single truth or common systems definition, it must also be meaningful *not* to have one, but to have a plurality instead. He argues that if it is meaningful to have a shared vision, it is equally meaningful to have a number of visions. The goal of dialogue does not need to be a unified understanding and a single master plan. It is possible to not have these and still generate an improved capacity for developing ideas and pursuing them into action while developing the complementarities of different institutions, organisations and activities.

Agoras for territorial development can lead to collective action, but do not necessarily do so. The consensus concept presented in Chapter 2 is not always an agreement on joint action, with a plan to execute jointly. It is a mutual understanding that can prevent certain processes from stagnation. It might be a mutual understanding of differences. That is why we use the term 'shared vision' differently to Gustavsen. We believe that a vision on the plurality and diversity of territorial actors can be a shared vision as long as participants are ready to mutually shape the understanding of the situation in a dialogue process. So dialogue in the agora is not necessarily a process that leads all participants to think the same. It is mutually shaping, which means that participants gain a better understanding of each other and that this influences their behaviour. This also fits with our interpretation of aligned action presented in Chapter 5. Action related to dialogue in the agora is not necessarily always joint action. Even in the absence of joint action, the mutual knowledge and understanding developed through dialogue in the agora contributes to territorial development through synergies in the behaviour of the actors.

---

4   A dialogue conference is a meeting between people organised and administrated by external resources such as an action researcher, but where it is the participants from the enterprises who constitute the main actors and resources (Gustavsen, 1992). The participants are a cross-section of the functions of an enterprise: line management, staff and experts, first line supervisors, employee representatives and one or two shopfloor workers without any representative role. In the dialogue conference the emphasis is on dialogue within the groups, not on invited speakers. Gustavsen therefore prefers not to have an opening statement beyond the essential message of the need for teamwork.

THE CONNECTION BETWEEN LANGUAGE AND ACTION

One of the most inspiring contributions from Gustavsen (1992) is his suggestion of how change happened in the LOM strategy. He argues that changes in patterns of communication are the spearhead in the change process. These new patterns of communication are, in turn, meant to lead to changes in the way the development work is conducted and in the amount of developmentally oriented work that is performed. The processes should then lead to new structures, mostly in work organisation and technology. In the LOM strategy, changes in work organisation are expected to come before changes in technology. Figure 6.1 shows an analytical model, but in practice the different steps are intermingled and it is not possible to separate them. Our proposal on how change happens in the agora is based on this framework. However, there are important differences between the workplace (Gustavsen's focus) and territories (our focus). In the case discussion we will adapt his model to territorial development.

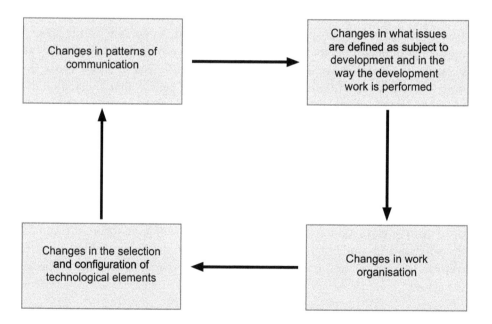

Figure 6.1   The change process in work organisation
Source: Gustavsen (1992), p. 70.

In his approach to language, and especially everyday language, Gustavsen builds on the work of the philosopher Ludwig Wittgenstein. According to Gustavsen (1992), in his later work about language theory Wittgenstein looked at what people say when they are transforming their physical world (Wittgenstein, 1953). The main argument is that language does not float freely in relation to practice. This implies that language cannot be restructured without a parallel restructuring of practice.

Gustavsen argues that there are many possible links between language and practice, and all suggest that language development and the development of new practice cannot be separated. Talking about the necessity for change in a specific practice is not enough. Gustavsen's (1992, p. 36) argument about language and change – that is, dialogue and development – focuses on the links between four elements: understanding, language, practice and construction of dialogues. He sees understanding as linked to language, which in turn is linked to practice. Language and understanding can be changed, but only by a mutually dependent development of language and practice, where the dependence is mediated by dialogue. The difference between action research and other approaches is that it considers all four of these elements, not just language.

Talk alone generates no change in practice. Gustavsen argues that the answer to avoiding the language trap is to:

> merge the research process with a restructuring of language. It might be argued that this is what social research generally does when concepts are defined and redefined, positioned in new ways in relation to each other, etc. If such a process is done by research alone it can, however, be likened to a linguistic game of patience where research sets the rules of the game. The game will then be meaningless to anyone else. The chief purpose of language however, is to link people to each other through the creation of shared meanings. If research wants to communicate outside the research community it is necessary to merge the research process with a process of restructuring of language which encompasses those who have to understand the research if the research is to become socially significant.
> (Gustavsen, 1992, p. 33)

Agoras are spaces where research has to reach out to a wider community than researchers alone. What we find inspiring in Gustavsen's approach is that he gives a clear message about the relevance of the shared construction of meaning between researchers and the public – in our case, policy makers. If such a process does not take place and researchers try to communicate with policy makers in the same language with which they communicate among themselves, their discourse will not be significant for those it is aimed at. No matter how concrete and focused the researchers might be, there are no short cuts in the agora. It is not possible to generate change without this initial construction of a shared language. This might sound obvious, but it seldom happens. And we should not be misled by the fact that researchers and policy makers often use the same words. If a shared meaning of discourse is not constructed, change will only happen on the surface of policy.

Another idea that has been useful for reflecting on our experience is *the challenge of scope*. It is not enough to participate in one case and then write an article and let the theory speak (Gustavsen, 1992). There is a need for active participation by researchers after 'the first case'. Gustavsen believes that it is necessary to share reflections through network-building and similar efforts which can bring a broad range of actors together to share ideas and practices. We believe that agoras for territorial development are spaces for such social construction processes. In this context, we agree with Gustavsen's argument that the issue is not identifying 'the best theory' in the abstract, but getting 'the right theory to the right place at the right time' (Gustavsen, 2001a). He argues that this is a problem of logistics. We believe this is the major challenge for theory in the agora.

DEMOCRATIC DIALOGUE AND DIALOGUE CONFERENCES

In Chapter 7 we will see that there is a strong link between the two authors who have inspired this part of the book, Bjørn Gustavsen and Paulo Freire. But there is a dimension where the perspectives of the authors seem to differ: the role of the researcher in the process. Gustavsen is explicit about his own political position when arguing that if the goal is to mobilise all concerned to pool their insight, synchronise their actions and ensure loyalty and support for decisions, there is no other social organisation comparable to participative democracy (Gustavsen, 1992, p. 120). However, the role of the researcher in dialogue conferences, which is the main tool he proposes for the development of dialogue, is not as explicitly political as in Freire's (1996; 2008a; 2008b) pedagogical method. (See also the discussion of Mode 2 knowledge cogeneration in Chapter 4.)

The role described for researchers in dialogue conferences is to help to organise the event, put together the report and sometimes to offer some comments. However, there is no research going on in parallel to the public proceedings. The conference report generally consists of the answers and statements summarising the group discussions, plus lists of participants and so forth. Modest interpretations are sometimes added, to the extent that the researcher believes that the interpretations will help move the process forward. Beyond this, the report contains no analysis (see Gustavsen 1992; 2001b; 2003). He also says that although research is welcome to make its contributions within specific fields related to the issue at stake (job design, for instance), these issues are not core ones in the kind of action research for which Gustavsen (2001b, p. 23) argues. Instead, the focus is on those dimensions of social organisation that decide the capacity for initiating, developing and putting ideas into effect. We will come back to these arguments in the case discussion.

Case: Gipuzkoa Sarean, Part 1[5]

Gipuzkoa Sarean is a project launched by the Provincial Council of Gipuzkoa and the Town Council of San Sebastian in 2009 with the aim of generating social capital to help improve competitiveness in the region (Barandiaran and Korta, 2011, p. 11). From the beginning it aimed to develop the soft elements of competitiveness related to social capital, such as networks, trust and collective knowledge and vision. This created a clear differentiation from the mainstream policy approaches traditionally used to construct advantage in that specific region. It was an innovative approach, and innovation is never easy. This was clear when the politicians in charge said that although they had the project in mind from the beginning of the legislature, they could not start it until they had implemented other projects with more traditional approaches to policy in order to gain credibility.

The main agora in the project which will be analysed in the case discussion was the direction board led by two policy makers and constituted of policy makers, researchers and those in charge of media communication.

From the beginning it was a project that aimed to combine research and action. Action research was formally considered as one of the approaches in the project; it was present in the discourse of some of the researchers and policy makers from the beginning, but there was no shared experience of action research among the participants (Gipuzkoa Sarean, 2009).

The period 2009–11 was used to assess social capital in the territory, and proposals for intervention based on the analysis were developed just before a

---

5   Part 2 of the case is presented in Chapter 7.

change in government. The analysis was based on a participatory process with 72 actors in the territory related to different aspects of competitiveness: firms, the knowledge system (schools, training centres, university and technology centres), the political system and associations with social aims (Barandiaran and Korta, 2011).

In 2011 new governments were formed in the city and the province. The new government's agenda in the provincial council included participation as a critical issue, and it wanted to continue with the project, redefining it to fit its own policies. In retrospect, and as we will argue later in this chapter, although they used some elements of the previous analysis and proposals for intervention, the main thing they retained from the previous phase was the agora – the space for mutual learning for policy makers and researchers.

From 2011 to the date of writing, there has been a continuous dialogue between policy makers and researchers. Some critical elements of the project have been kept and many others have been redefined. With the new government in Gipuzkoa, various reflection and policy design spaces have been created that have configured the agora in a different way. The change in government in 2011 has given us the opportunity to define the two different stages and reflect on how the agora has evolved in each of them.

Case Discussion: The Democratic Agora

In this discussion we will reflect on what conditions are needed to create an agora that works. We begin with an argument which is the result of combining the discussions presented in Parts I and II of this book. It is thus the result of some years of action and reflection on territorial development. We argue that what makes agoras work is dialogue, but not just any dialogue. Contexts of territorial complexity (see Chapter 2) require dialogue processes that are democratic in the terms defined by Gustavsen. This is because hierarchy is not the main pattern of relationship among autonomous actors in the territory. We could describe an agora that does not work as a place where researchers and policy makers meet and the result is a sum of different (often contradictory) knowledge that generates a lot of talk that is very difficult to convert into action. We have been part of many processes of this type. We see an agora that works as a space where researchers and policy makers meet and the result is a process where they cogenerate collective knowing (see Chapter 3).

With this argument in mind, and using the concepts proposed by Gustavsen, we approach the discussion of GS by focusing on the two different stages demarcated by the change in government. We must confess to the reader that there was a moment in the reflection and writing process when we felt tempted to caricaturise the discussion, to say that at one stage there was no democratic dialogue, and in the process we were able to construct it. We could then have made a clear-cut argument about the differences. But our conclusion is that it is not so easy to label these situations. An agora that fulfils the conditions for democratic dialogue proposed by Gustavsen is an ideal agora – one we will probably not find in practice. We are aware of this in the discussion that follows when we use the concept of the *democratic agora* – an agora that fulfils Gustavsen's conditions for democratic dialogue. Although the concept points to an ideal horizon, we will develop the discussion by trying to focus on a practical perspective while retaining the nuances and complexity of the case.

We will begin the discussion by focusing on how to start the change process Gustavsen proposes in his framework; more specifically, we will analyse the first step: *change in patterns of communication*. We understand that the creation of a democratic agora begins with a change in patterns of communication between researchers and practitioners. This should then lead to a new agenda for development (see Figure 6.1).

GIPUZKOA SAREAN: CHANGING PATTERNS OF COMMUNICATION

In the initial stages, the communication pattern in the direction group of Gipuzkoa Sarean was centralised. There were two policy makers who led the process, with one as the central node for most of the communication in the project. Three research teams were participating in the process, but communication among researchers also took place through the directors of the project.

Action research had been accepted as the approach for the project in the formal strategy document, but it soon became clear that there were very different approaches to research within the project. The policy maker acting as the central node had research experience and a very clear idea of the process in his mind, and he directly instructed the different research teams on what they should deliver in terms of questionnaires, data and reports.

In the initial stage, communication between policy makers and researchers was defined mostly in terms of instructions from policy makers on what they needed, and the researchers delivering databases and reports with an analysis of social capital in the area. If we look back on projects where we have worked with policy makers, this could be considered quite a common pattern of communication, particularly in projects funded by policy makers to address a specific challenge.

In its initial stage, the direction group of GS was an agora. But did it fulfil Gustavsen's criteria for a democratic agora? We will consider this from two angles. The first concerns the status of participants (the fourth of Gustavsen's principles for democratic dialogue). We definitely did not have the same status. Our experience is that our projects as researchers have mostly fallen into two categories: projects launched by policy makers where decision capacity is kept on the policy side, and projects launched by researchers where they involve policy makers mainly as a source of data but the researchers decide on the design and development of the project. The origins of the funds used determine the pattern. Usually, policy makers shape the projects they are funding with a specific policy goal in mind. Researchers shape those projects that are directly funded as research, with no specific policy makers directly using the results. If a balance in status is needed in democratic agoras, the way research is funded could be hindering democratic agoras.

The other angle, which is closely linked to the previous one, is whether the ordinary work roles of the participants are among the issues subject to discussion (the eleventh of Gustavsen's principles for democratic dialogue). This item could be the answer to the challenge posed by the previous angle. Few agoras begin as democratic agoras, but through dialogue and discussion of the roles played by everyone in the process, they may become more democratic.

If we return to the case with this discussion in mind, we can see that when the project developed and there was more activity, this created pressure on the policy maker who had the vision and was guiding the decision making. He, helped by the other policy maker and a civil servant, had been at the core of every critical decision in the process on both policy and research issues. At this stage in the process he proposed creating a new function (role) in the project: research director. The new director did not have the same status in the project as the two policy directors, but it definitely brought about change in the patterns of communication in the project. One of us (authors) took on this role. In parallel, one of the civil servants was appointed as the person in charge of operational issues, and the role of the technical secretariat was reinforced to support both.

The research director opened a direct dialogue with other researchers in the project and felt more confident in presenting proposals from the research team to the policy directors. The pattern of communication also changed in relation to the first of Gustavsen's principles (a relationship of give and take). Researchers were not only giving the answers policy makers had asked for, they were also posing their own questions. The status of researchers and policy makers had become more equal.

When we tried to understand what had happened to patterns of communication in the change process, the answer always pointed to the same concept: social capital, and more specifically, trust. This means that in most projects, where researchers and policy makers have no previous experience of working together, it is difficult to begin as a democratic agora. It takes time to develop social capital. Democratic dialogue cannot be designed on paper and implemented; it requires the construction of social capital, and this is a medium/long-term process.

Agoras are not an automatic development, they are the result of a long-term process of construction we described in terms of social capital in Chapter 3. This is consistent with Gustavsen's approach when he says that 'change is dependent upon trust between the parties involved' (Gustavsen, 2008, p. 429).

Returning to the change process in GS, the provincial council election in 2011 resulted in a new government, which led to a new stage of the project. The agora presented to the new government was the one at the end of the previous stage, with a political direction, an academic director and a technical secretariat. The continuity of the project depended on the new government's decision to make the project its own. The project depended completely on funding from the political team, and researchers had no input on its continuity. Again, the distance in status between researchers and practitioners grew and the need for social capital was evident.

Dialogue slowly developed, mainly led by the civil servant who had been given responsibility for the project in the previous phase. The cabinet of the general deputy leading the project invited all deputies (ministers) and their teams to the agora. During the first year a team of five researchers and about ten policy makers regularly participated in the dialogue. The agora was now more diverse, both in terms of researchers and practitioners. Proposals were coming from a diversity of participants in the agora, and the researchers' proposals were integrated with those of the practitioners. However, the authority to make decisions on the continuity of the project was still concentrated in the hands of policy makers.

THE CONSTRUCTION OF A SHARED LANGUAGE IN THE AGORA

Before embarking on a deeper analysis of the challenges posed in the previous discussion, we will share some examples of how language was constructed in the agora with the new government. We will see how the balance in status of researchers and policy makers influenced the construction of language and – as in Gustavsen's framework for change – the agenda for development. We will use three examples of construction of shared meaning. These are related to the terms *competitiveness/territorial development*, *social capital* and *agora*.

When the project began in 2009, policy makers had already defined it as a project to develop *social capital* to generate *competitiveness*. We (both authors of this book) were asked to write a strategic document for the project for the kick-off meeting. We had agreed with policy makers that we would use an AR approach, and the main features of AR had been discussed. In the document and kick-off meeting we mainly emphasised the methodological side of the process. The document presented some discussions about the fields of competitiveness and social capital, but offered no interpretation of what these concepts meant in the project. The feedback we received both from policy makers and other researchers was that we should state what competitiveness and social capital meant in the project. We proposed a series of discussions between researchers and policy makers to construct this shared meaning, but this did not happen. We argued that our role was to pose the questions, not to give the answers, but our status in the process was not solid enough to keep this issue open for discussion. We had included it in the strategy document, but lacked the social capital to take democratic dialogue from paper to practice.

The absence of mutually shaped meaning also affected the interpretation of *social capital* and *intervention on social capital* in the project. One approach was that social capital was beneficial for competitiveness, and intervention should have the goal of developing the critical pillars of social capital in the territory. The other approach, inspired by action research, was that the process should start with the definition of problems we wanted to address (see the discussion in Chapter 4 and Figure 4.3). Only then should a reflection on how social capital could help to solve such problems take place. These divergent perceptions coexisted in the project, hindering it until a new researcher entered the process and raised the issue. She had a strong international reputation and argued for the need to have a clear agreement on what social capital was needed for, as it was neither good nor bad in itself. Her position was accepted by the policy makers and researchers in the project, helping to construct a shared vision on the issue. We have argued that funding has a critical influence on status in projects. Authority based on a recognised trajectory in a research field does too. However, bringing well-known researchers into projects is not enough. There were other researchers with much recognition in the field involved in the project, but they did not contribute to the construction of shared meaning as effectively. A key difference was that they communicated mainly through speeches and none had entered into dialogue in the agora as she did.

When the change in government took place, the definitions of competitiveness and social capital immediately emerged in the discussion between policy makers and researchers. The new government decided to replace the concept of competitiveness with that of territorial development. Following that decision, two experts in this field became more deeply involved in the research team. A series of workshops were developed based on the frameworks proposed by these researchers, and a shared discourse on territorial development was constructed in the agora. Territorial development in GS meant 'a process of mobilisation and participation of different actors (public and private) in which they discuss and agree on strategies that can lead individual and collective actions' (Gipuzkoa Sarean, 2012a, Alburquerque, 2012). Consistent with Gustavsen's (1992) framework for change, this definition influenced not only what issues were defined as subject to development, but also the way the development work was to be performed.

We now present the discussion on social capital. The new politicians were reluctant to use the term 'capital' as a central concept for the project. However, they still considered the concept important, particularly for the development of trust. The head of cabinet of the general deputy had said that what they needed was to build bridges – some old bridges that had been broken in the past, and other new bridges that were necessary to face the future. This discourse led the researchers to see analogies between social capital and building bridges, and an agreement was made that the discourse of the project would develop in terms of building bridges when communicating with other actors in the territory. Researchers would continue to use social capital in their academic production. This is an example of how the decision on what concepts to apply, their content as well as the relationships between them, has to be settled in each case (Gustavsen, 2008, p. 425).

Finally, *agora,* the core concept in this book, was also part of the dialogue process. When it was suggested by researchers as a space where policy makers and researchers worked together, policy makers showed interest. They wanted to better understand what the agora was. When the discussion ended, they agreed that it was an adequate concept for the project, but they wanted to find a name for it that would be more significant locally. They reflected on what, in the culture of the territory, would be closest to the Greek *agora,* and the term *plaza* was chosen. Language was being locally adapted.

THINKING BEYOND SPECIFIC AGORAS

In the previous section we reflected on change in patterns of communication and shared construction of language as stages of change in the agora. We discussed the relevance of status and found some taken-for-granted assumptions that shaped status in the agora. We believe that there are frameworks defined at regional and national levels that were determinant in such taken-for-granted assumptions. We will focus the rest of the discussion on this issue.

We depart from the difference in status between policy makers and researchers.[6] We have seen that the building of social capital can balance status, making cogeneration easier and approaching the fulfilment of the criteria for democratic dialogue. But social capital in a specific dialogue process is not enough. We argue that there is a glass ceiling (a limiting factor that is not always evident) for social capital in concrete agoras because of the way decisions are made about the role of research and the use of research funds in wider contexts (science and research policy at regional and national level).

Our reflection on the glass ceiling builds on one main contradiction. Democratic dialogue criteria propose that the role of everyone is subject to discussion in the agora. But the discussion in the agora seldom includes discussion of the elements that are influencing how research is understood and funded in the region or country. Thus, dialogue in the agora seldom touches on issues that are critical for transforming dialogue into democratic dialogue.

There are very strong taken-for-granted principles on the role of researchers in different regions and countries. The issues relating to funding and the status of researchers in a territory are not defined from scratch in each agora.

---

6   The case we are using in this chapter is one where policy makers are funding the project and
     have the final say on its continuity, but as we said earlier, there are research-driven projects
     where it is the other way round. The discussion applies to both situations.

Many of the frameworks are discussed in spaces (research councils, university management and departmental structures and so on) that are not the same as the agoras where researchers and policy makers develop specific territorial development projects. This is why, by the time a specific process of dialogue starts in an agora for territorial development, some basic conditions are frequently taken for granted. In GS we discussed our roles and status, but there was a limiting factor that was never questioned: those funding the project were making the final decisions that affected both action and research.

We now want to move the discussion on democratic agoras in a direction that is more provocative than operational. We think that democratic agoras are spaces where both researchers and policy makers have the status to decide on the funding and continuity of the project. This does not mean they have the same role in the decision process, but that they have mechanisms to share the decision making. The basic justification for this is that the projects developed in the agora, when genuinely cogenerative, are both policy and research. Consequently, to become democratic, agoras need to integrate a dialogue on the scientific and research policy in the territory and overcome the factors that constrict them.

That is why the demarcation of a democratic agora is wider than the one we have often had in mind. We often considered the actors affected by the issue at stake in one single research project, but we seldom included the actors related to the issue through the definition of science and research policy at regional or national level. Until this point, the policy makers and researchers defining the general frameworks for science and research were not on our agenda. We believe that connections between both types of territorial actors should be sought.

THE CHALLENGE OF MAKING REGIONAL AND NATIONAL RESEARCH POLICY VISIBLE IN AGORAS

Bringing the national and regional research frameworks into debate in micro processes is not an easy challenge. This should be done not only in the agoras where scientific and research policy are defined, but in a diversity of agoras where researchers and policy makers interact. A critical awareness of how the research priorities are established should be part of the discussion in every agora, as these frameworks – often defined at regional and national levels – later influence every micro process establishing the glass ceiling mentioned above.

The agora is a public space of mutual shaping. But we know that not all processes in which researchers and policy makers shape research policy are public, nor are they beyond self-interest and power play. By developing the concept of a democratic agora based on action research, we propose bringing part of the dialogue that usually develops in a private sphere to the public.

We will now use Eikeland (2006) to shape this argument and propose the agora as a space that helps to connect what goes on in public and 'onstage' with what happens 'backstage'.[7] This relates to the discussion in Chapter 2 about the need to keep dialogue going even when it is not possible to do so in the formal spaces of the agora. The formal part of the process is the onstage aspect of the agora. According to Eikeland (2006, p. 229), onstage we perform our roles and appointed tasks. Backstage we discuss and critically analyse experiences from performing onstage, we practise to improve, we switch roles and plays and so on. According to Eikeland, the backstage space must become a counter-public sphere, protecting people from the rhetorical forces at work in the public sphere. We believe that backstage is part of the agora and needs to be understood if we want to understand territorial development. This might seem to contradict the definition of the agora as a public space. We believe that when backstage and onstage are connected and what was learnt backstage is later shared onstage, the contradiction disappears. Not every process can bear the pressure generated onstage. Backstage spaces are needed in order to develop what will in the future be shared in the public sphere. By focusing mainly on structured environments for knowledge cogeneration or by giving centrality to events such as dialogue and search conferences in the construction of arenas for dialogue, we might underestimate the relevance of the processes going on backstage.

Our argument is that many debates on regional and national science and research policy take place backstage, without the participation of actors that later work in agoras for territorial development. Agoras for territorial development should not only consider the formal discourse played out onstage by those defining regional and national science and research policy. An effort should be made to share part of the discussions going on backstage so that agoras become spaces where these debates are gradually made public, discussed and connected to action. This would contribute to overcoming the limitations for democratic dialogue in agoras.

---

7   Eikeland (2006, p. 230) uses the term 'offstage' for social research as interpreting audience and spectator. This connects with the position we have discussed of the social researcher as outsider to territorial development agoras.

Closing Comments

Gustavsen proposed his framework of change to help reflect on the workplace. The concepts of *pattern of communication* and *issues defined as subjects of development* helped us to reflect on a context of territorial development. But finding concepts that can mirror the concepts of *work organisation* and *technological elements* in territorial development is a challenge. We will now reflect on the changes produced in GS to propose such concepts.

The definition of territorial development as a process of mobilisation and participation by the provincial council led to the need for a specific type of relationship with the actors of the territory that were to be mobilised and expected to participate. The need for a new mode of governance in the territory emerged. In order to be consistent with their discourse and gain credibility with the actors, the new mode of governance needed to influence the council's policy programmes.

Although GS is still an ongoing process at the time of writing, the new concept of territorial development is already being applied in practice. In the meetings for policy design, Gustavsen's framework was discussed by researchers and policy makers. The concept that replaced *changes in work organisation* was *changes in territorial governance*. The concept that replaced *changes in the selection and configuration of technological elements* was *changes in the selection and configuration of policy tools*.

The result of the cogenerative process has been the proposal of an adaptation of Gustavsen's (1992) framework suitable for territorial development (see Figure 6.2). We believe the new framework helps us to understand how agoras for territorial development can be much more than just talk, generating change processes that can create new modes of governance and new approaches to policy making.

We argued that a democratic agora, with all 13 principles of Gustavsen (1992) fulfilled, is difficult and probably in most cases impossible to attain. However, this does not mean that we should not work towards achieving a democratic agora. It is the *process* of pursuing a democratic agora that generates territorial development.

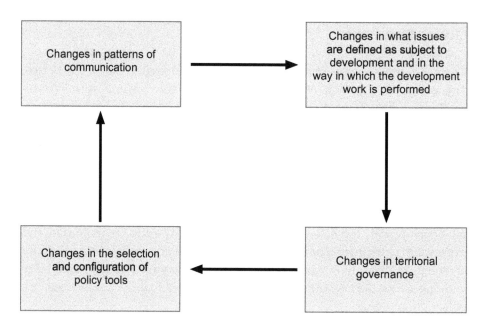

Figure 6.2   The change process in territorial development
Source: Adapted from Gustavsen (1992).

7

The Pedagogical Process in the Agora

In June 2010 we taught on a master's course in Territorial Development in Rafaela, Argentina. When we were introduced to the students, we noticed that the group was different to the student groups we were used to. Among the students we met were the Technical Secretary of the Chamber of Commerce, researchers and managers from the local university, managers from the development agency and competitiveness programme, managers and researchers from technology centres, representatives of a local institute for training and studies on territorial development, a provincial deputy and a broad group from the municipality, including representatives of urbanism, development, innovation and international relations, human resources, employment and social economy, management and participation and relationships with neighbouring areas. In the classroom we were struck by the way abstract discussion of concepts was combined with a discussion of the actual development of Rafaela. Students did not look at the issues discussed from the outside but positioned as insiders. They were problem owners in the learning process.

The following year we returned to Rafaela to learn more. Meanwhile, we had read Paulo Freire's work. We had begun to think about our experience from an educational perspective. This chapter is a result of that reflection process.

Most researchers in territorial development have teaching responsibilities and have discussed the third role of the university: territorial development[1] (see, for example, Chatterton and Goddard, 2000; Etzkowitz and Leydesdorff, 2001). This role is generating value for the society we are part of (OECD, 2011). But we have found few discussions on the pedagogical dimension of the third role and how this role involves a political position of the researcher/teacher.

---

1   The two other roles of a university are teaching and research.

This chapter will mainly focus on the educational process in the agora. The closing comments will consider formal university courses as potential agoras for territorial development. In this chapter we will focus on a single author, Paulo Freire. After connecting Freire to Gustavsen through the concept of dialogue, we will discuss three core ideas. The first is that the educational process in the agora cannot be understood as a process where knowledge is passed on to those who learn by those who know. We will discuss the meanings of *banking education* and *problem-posing education*. Second, we will show that a problem-posing approach to the agora requires careful design. We will argue that researchers cannot design the learning process of policy makers on their own, even when they think they understand what policy makers need. Finally, we will see that using the approach proposed by Freire is not a matter of technically mastering a method. Researcher neutrality is not possible in such an educational process, and the researcher brings his or her ideological background to the process.

With these concepts in mind, we will continue with the discussion of GS, the project for territorial development introduced in Chapter 6. We will also talk about the case of Rafaela. This case was used by researchers and policy makers in GS to reflect on their own process. It is this interpretation of Rafaela used in GS, not the Rafaela case itself, that we will consider here.

The following section will present an approach to the educational process in the agora, based on Freire's work. We will go through his approaches to dialogue, the problem-posing method, the pedagogical process and the impossibility of neutrality for the researcher. After presenting some more data about the GS case, we will begin the case discussion by considering the banking approach in territorial development and the ideological connection to change. We will end the chapter with some closing comments on the role of the university in territorial development.

The Pedagogical Approach to the Agora

This chapter builds on Paulo Freire's pedagogical approach, presented in *Pedagogy of the Oppressed* in 1970 (Freire, 1996) and revisited by the author himself 22 years later in *Pedagogy of Hope* (Freire, 2008a). Freire's pedagogy was based on his experiences in Brazil and Chile, and the experiences that have led us to write this book differ substantially from his. However, elements of his pedagogy have inspired our approach to the agora.

For Freire, the pedagogy of the oppressed, as a humanist and libertarian pedagogy, has two distinct stages. In the first, the oppressed unveil the world of oppression and through the praxis commit themselves to its transformation. In the second stage, in which the reality of oppression has already been transformed, this pedagogy ceases to belong to the oppressed and becomes a pedagogy of all people in the process of permanent liberation. In both stages, it is always through in-depth action that the culture of domination is culturally confronted. In the first stage this confrontation occurs through a change in the way the oppressed perceive the world of oppression; in the second stage it occurs through the expulsion of the myths created and developed in the old order (Freire, 1996, p. 36).

As mentioned above, *Pedagogy of Hope* (Freire, 2008a) is a revisit in which Freire refers to *Pedagogy of the Oppressed* as a book 'written with anger, with love. Without this there is no hope. It is a defense of tolerance and radicalism; a critic to sectarianism, an understanding of the progressive postmodernism and a rejection of the conservative, neoliberal' (Freire, 2008a, p. 26). Freire says that his revisit of *Pedagogy of the Oppressed* does not lead him to talk about what happened, but about what is happening. He does so with the belief that *Pedagogy of the Oppressed* is as needed 22 years later as it was when published (Freire, 2008a, p. 214).

His language – in terms of the oppressor and the oppressed – is not our language when we refer to territorial development. But when we have worked with practitioners in change processes that aimed to create more collaborative innovation policies, we have found patterns of behaviour that can be described effectively using the frameworks proposed by Freire. The literature on territorial development and innovation systems has often left out a discussion of power, which has perhaps been viewed as an issue to be addressed by political science. It is beyond the scope of this chapter to address such a discourse directly. But we are aware that by avoiding this discourse, learning has been considered a fairly mechanical endeavour – an operative process once we have someone who has knowledge and someone else who needs to learn. Learning has been assumed to be a matter of transferring knowledge from one to the other. But learning in democratic agoras for territorial development is connected to action, and consequently to change in behaviour. Change in behaviour is not a matter of obtaining knowledge from those who have it. It is a matter of changing our inner beliefs, confronting our fears and changing the status of different actors in a process. That is why we propose avoiding a simplistic approach to learning in the agora by exploring the educational process as Freire develops it.

As mentioned above, our context and language are different from Freire's, but there is a concept that is at the core of Freire's approach to pedagogy that we want to rescue for the agora. This is the concept of *awareness*, which is the result of unveiling reality. Its meaning and process will be presented throughout the following sections.

Dialogue: The Core Process in the Agora

In his *Pedagogy of Hope*, Freire shares some criticisms he has received about his writing style. In response, he argues that the aesthetic moment of language must be sought by all, whether we are rigorous scientists or not. There is no incompatibility between rigour in the search for understanding of the world and beauty in the way we express discoveries (Freire, 2008a, pp. 94–5).

As a small tribute to this argument, we will adapt our writing style in this section and use quotes from *Pedagogy of the Oppressed* that aim to retain the beauty of the way Freire expressed his discoveries. We are also aware that Freire's writing style and his very personal use of language have shaped the way we have written the sections of this chapter dealing with his work, where we stick to the exact words he used and have adopted a much more literal approach to presenting his work than in the rest of the book.[2]

Like Gustavsen, Freire underlines the role of the construction of language in the dialogue process. The construction of language is present in the following:

> *As we attempt to analyse dialogue as a human phenomenon, we discover something which is the essence of dialogue itself, the word. But the word is more than just an instrument which makes dialogue possible; accordingly, we must seek its constitutive elements. Within the word we find two dimensions, reflection and action, in such a radical interaction that if one is sacrificed –even in part- the other immediately suffers. There is no true word that is not at the same time a praxis. Thus, to speak a true word is to transform the world.*
>
> *(Freire, 1996, p. 68)*

---

2   The edition we have used was translated into English by Myra Bergman Ramos.

To change language is part of the process of changing the world. The relationship language-thought-world is a dialectical relationship, evolving, contradictory.

(Freire, 2008a, p. 90)

The link between action and reflection, which we have presented mostly through the contributions of Greenwood and Levin (2007) and Gustavsen (1992), is also developed by Freire in this paragraph:

To exist, humanly, is to 'name' the world, to change it. Once named, the world in its turn reappears to the namers as a problem and requires of them a new naming. Human beings are not built in silence, but in word, in work, in action-reflection.

(Freire, 1996, p. 69)

Gustavsen's approach to broad and direct participation is also present in Freire:

But while to say the true word – which is work, which is praxis - is to transform the world, saying that word is not the privilege of some few persons, but the right of everyone. Consequently, no one can say a true word alone – nor can she say it for another, in a prescriptive act which robs others of their words.

(Freire, 1996, p. 69)

The link between dialogue and the pedagogical approach is made in the following:

If it is in the speaking their word that people, by naming the world, transform it, dialogue imposes itself as the way by which they achieve significance as human beings. Dialogue is thus an existential necessity. And since dialogue is the encounter in which the united reflection and action of the dialoguers are addressed to the world which is to be transformed and humanized, this dialogue cannot be reduced to the act of one person's 'depositing' ideas in another, nor can it become a simple exchange of ideas to be 'consumed' by the discussants.

(Freire, 1996, pp. 69–70)

The Problem-posing Method

By introducing the pedagogical approach in the agora, we do not aim to set aside the concept of action research we have been using as the core of our approach. Freire's approach to pedagogy is completely consistent with the concept of action research. It is, as a matter of fact, classified as a specific branch of action research (Greenwood and Levin, 2007). What we will do with the pedagogical approach is to explore deeply how action research can have an influence on the inner frameworks that shape the way participants in a process understand the world and relate to it. Freire (2008a, p. 30) himself says that there is no teaching without research or research without teaching.

Freire affirms that education is suffering from narration sickness (Freire, 1996, pp. 52–3). Narration, with the teacher as narrator, leads students to mechanically memorise the narrated content. Education thus becomes an act of depositing, in which the students are the depositories and the teacher is the depositor. This is the *banking concept of education*, and it represents the concept of linear transfer of knowledge from researchers to policy makers we discussed in Chapter 4. Freire believes that education must begin with the solution of the teacher–student contradiction so that both are simultaneously teachers and students. In the agora, this means that both researchers and policy makers are responsible for mutual learning.

Freire proposes the *problem-posing method* as an alternative to the banking approach. Students presented with problems relating to themselves will feel increasingly challenged and obliged to respond to those challenges. This happens because they apprehend each challenge as interrelated to other problems within the context, not as a theoretical question (Freire, 1996, p. 62). In problem-posing education, people develop their capacity to critically perceive the way they exist in the world. The form of action they adopt is to a large extent a function of this perception (Freire, 1996, p. 64).

For Freire, awareness is a critical concept for linking dialogue and action. Dialogue is indispensable to unveiling reality. The awareness of their situation leads people to apprehend that situation as a historical reality susceptible to transformation, and this shapes action (Freire, 1996, p. 66).

In the agora for territorial development, dialogue brings researchers and policy makers together to perceive themselves both as part of the problem they face and as part of the solution when they understand problems as a process they can transform. We argue that it is this concept of awareness that includes self-awareness that drives the difference between using the same words and cogenerating the path to territorial development.

Together with awareness and self-awareness, the concept of *thematic universe* is critical to understanding Freire's proposed pedagogical process. In order to decide on the themes of education, Freire proposes investigating people's thematic universe – the complexity of their 'generative themes', the issues that are relevant to understanding both the context of the participants and their perception of the context, to avoid banking approaches (Freire, 1996, pp. 77–8). The generative themes are found in the thought-language with which men and women refer to reality, the levels at which they perceive that reality and their view of the world. Freire emphasises that the generative theme cannot be found in people, divorced from reality; nor yet in reality, divorced from people; much less in 'no man's land' (Freire, 1996, pp. 87–8). When Freire argues that it is not possible to understand these themes apart from people and that it is necessary for those concerned to understand them as well, we find the connection with the cogenerative process in the agora. As for him, thematic investigation becomes a common striving towards awareness of reality and self-awareness, which makes investigation a starting point for the educational process.

Awareness is thus a central element in the agora. The change in reality cannot begin until our (researchers' and practitioners') perception of it is unveiled and understood and we see that we need to change in order to change the world. As long as researchers think they know the solutions to policy makers' problems and policy makers think they know what they need from researchers, change will be hindered. It is in the shared, dialogical understanding of the frameworks of others that the change process can start. This is not only a process of discovery about others, it is also a process of self-discovery. We are often unaware of what we ourselves are taking for granted.

Coding and Decoding for Awareness

Freire proposes developing an educational process with a problem-posing approach. By discussing this, we will gain a more concrete perspective on how the critical awareness previously discussed can be constructed. The process is complementary to Gustavsen's framework of change, and it is not difficult to think of the following method in terms of our research processes, no matter how explicit the educational goal is in them.

For Freire, the discovery of generative themes (the issues that are relevant for the participants) is a sequence of coding and decoding processes. The educator (researcher in the agora) approaches the field and codifies certain situations after observing them and opening a dialogue with some actors in the field. The codification must not be too explicit about the perceptions of the researcher, but must be clear enough to let the participants in the process talk about the issue.[3] When confronted with this codification, the participants collaborating with researchers in this preliminary phase decode it, talking about it and generating data that will lead to an interpretation of how the participants perceive the specific issue.

This method does not involve reducing the concrete to the abstract by codifying it, but rather maintains both elements as opposites which interrelate dialectically in the reflection process. In this way, the issue moves from the abstract to the concrete and from the concrete to the abstract (Freire, 1996, p. 86). This means that the process is not finished when concrete situations are presented in terms of a codification, but the codification is discussed in terms of concrete experiences, and it is by repeating this process that awareness emerges.

If we interpret the agora in terms of Freire's method, we find that the task of the researcher working on the relevant issues in the agora is to 're-present' these issues to the people from whom she or he first received them, and to 're-present' them not as a lecture, but as a problem (Freire, 1996, p. 90). When decoding this representation, the territorial actors tend to take the step from the representation to the very concrete situation in which they find themselves. Through this process, reality ceases to look like a blind alley and takes on its true aspect: a challenge which human beings must meet (Freire, 1996, p. 86).

This coding and decoding process is necessary in order to gain awareness. Researchers might feel tempted to avoid it in a first stage when they become familiar with the contradictions of territorial actors in the agora. But this initial understanding does not authorise researchers to begin to structure what Freire calls the *programme content* of the educational action and what we call the *agenda for development* in the agora. This is because previous to

---

3   Freire used drawings to codify situations.

the coding and decoding process this initial understanding of reality is still the researchers' perception, not that of the people (territorial actors) (Freire, 1996, p. 95).

In many research processes where this coding and decoding sequence is missing, researchers construct their output in terms of reports, training materials or papers after the first codification. This has to do with the understanding of research outputs as a product, and not as a process. For Freire, the coding and decoding process aims to prepare training materials to be used in a new dialogical process. Similarly, in the agora the research outputs of coding and decoding should again be integrated into the dialogue with the actors. It is as the result of this process that collective knowing is constructed.

The Impossibility of Neutrality for the Researcher

Carlos Núñez Hurtado, in his prologue to *Pedagogy of Hope*, says that Paulo Freire once told him: 'I am substantively political and only adjectively pedagogist' (Freire, 2008a, p. 18).

The educator Freire conceives as participating in the processes we have described is a political actor. Freire says that:

> *A moment comes when it is not possible to exist without being subject to the radical and deep tension between good and bad, between dignity and indignity, between decency and shamelessness, between the beauty and ugliness of the world. This means that it is not possible to exist without educators assuming their right or duty to choose, to decide, to fight, to do politics.*
>
> (Freire, 2008b, p. 51)

He also says that all educational practice demands the existence of subjects, objects and also goals, dreams, utopia, ideals. This is the cause of its political quality, of not being capable of being neutral (Freire, 2008b, p. 67). We argue that the researcher who enters a policy learning process with policy makers is not neutral. However, his or her political role has seldom been discussed, and what discussion there has been has mostly been critical. We also argue that the agora has the quality of being political, like Freire's educational practice.

We assert that no researcher in the agora is neutral, no matter what research method is used. In the words of Freire, nobody can be in this world, with the world and with others in a neutral way. Nobody can be there 'just checking'. We cannot study the world without engagement as if suddenly, mysteriously, we had nothing to do with it (Freire, 2008b, p. 74). For Freire, education is a form of intervention (Freire, 2008b, p. 93). For us, research in the agora is a form of intervention as well.

The political role of researchers might be approached with suspicion by many. Freire's arguments depart from the statement that the reading of the world cannot be the reading of the academics imposed on the popular classes. In our case it would be the reading of academics imposed on policy makers. But he also says that the dialectical and democratic position implies the intervention of the intellectual as a necessary condition, and there is no betrayal of democracy in this (Freire, 2008a, p. 133). Thus, Freire poses a challenge for researchers, as we cannot approach the field with a reading of the territory that is the truth, but nor can we approach it without a political position.

Case: Gipuzkoa Sarean, Part 2

We now return to the case of Gipuzkoa Sarean. This time, we focus on the period after the new government took over in 2011. It took time for the new team to familiarise themselves with the project. The fact that the first formal meeting of all researchers and policy makers was a workshop where they discussed the main concepts of the project (territorial development, participation, social capital, action research) shaped the future patterns of communication. From that moment on, it seemed natural to continue with a series of workshops in which these concepts were discussed in depth, responding to frameworks contributed by different researchers in the team.

A wide range of members of the government representing different departments participated in these discussions. Most of them viewed the workshops as training processes where they could learn and discuss concepts related to territorial development with experts in the field. The workshops were combined with meetings of a smaller group of researchers and politicians in the general deputy's cabinet, with a more operational perspective on how this vision of territorial development could be incorporated into concrete policy processes in the territory.

During 2012 a new approach to territorial development was defined, mainly based in Latin American experiences brought to the project by researchers working there (Alburquerque et al., 2008). The main Latin American experience shared with policy makers was the case of Rafaela. After discussing it, and inspired by what had been going on in Rafaela, various members of the government expressed a wish to generate a space for learning that would evolve towards a space for co-ordination of policy. This was the core idea that led us to interpret the agora as a pedagogical process and integrate Freire's approach into GS.

The next step was a discussion on how to evolve from learning to policy intervention. The researcher facilitating this discussion suggested that it was not possible to go directly from the learning going on in workshops to intervention. It was too big a jump. He proposed the discussion of three possible spaces in the agora (see Figure 7.1).

The space for learning was conceived as what had already been happening in GS: workshops where researchers and policy makers had discussed the main concepts in the project and what they meant for the group. The space for intervention was understood as the dialogue the policy makers wanted to open with the actors in the territory, to construct the newly-defined participatory approach to territorial development. Our challenge (policy makers and researchers) was to construct the intermediate space, the space for policy design, where the ideas discussed in the space for learning could be transformed into concrete projects and processes to be shared with the territorial actors.

The discussion led to a new stage in the project, where reflection was brought from the space for learning to the space for co-ordination and policy design by approaching the discussion of what we wanted to change and how we were going to generate change. Only after these issues were discussed did we define a concrete annual work plan, running to 2013. The reflection of the research team after these discussions, later shared with policy makers, was that the three spaces were part of the agora, they were part of the dialogue between researchers and practitioners, but each had their own goals and composition of actors. Each required their own methods and approaches. The democratic agora defined in Chapter 6 was thus configuring not as one space, but as a combination of different spaces where different actors in the policy process participated and where the dialogue between the abstract and the concrete presented by Freire was shaped differently.

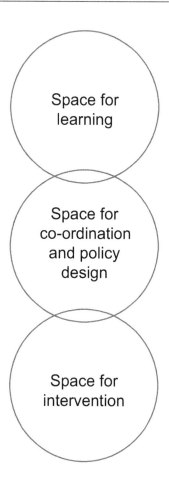

Figure 7.1   Three possible spaces in Gipuzkoa Sarean
Source: Costamagna, P., Gipuzkoa Sarean Workshop, 27 June 2012.

Case Discussion: Constructing Spaces for Awareness

AVOIDING THE BANKING APPROACH IN TERRITORIAL DEVELOPMENT

For the discussion presented in this section we build on the description of the case we made in Chapter 6, but we use Freire's concepts to reflect on it. The main issue addressed is that even in cases where researchers and practitioners apparently meet in democratic agoras that take into consideration the criteria proposed by Gustavsen, we might be replicating banking approaches.

In the initial stage of GS with the first government there was a deep questioning of how policy was defined and there was an ambitious project to introduce the concept of social capital as an approach that would add an innovative dimension to policy making. But this was mainly the vision of one of the directors of the project. This vision was communicated in the agora, but there was no process that resembled Freire's method of coding and decoding for the rest of the participants to unveil the meaning of it and connect the process to our own experiences. Some of us worked for two years with this politician with the feeling that we couldn't properly help in the project because we were unable to grasp what he had in his mind.

There was once a conversation between one of the policy makers and one of us. The policy maker, after listening to one of our presentations in a workshop told us 'but you have changed, you talked different today from how you used to talk', and he made us reflect to answer 'yes, it is through our own change process that we can generate change in others'. This was one of the few moments when a clearer awareness seemed to be emerging in the meetings of the direction board. But this perspective did not get further. Meanwhile we had an ongoing feeling that social capital was not adequately conceptualised in the process. We assumed that this was the reason why it was difficult for us to understand what was expected from us. We tried to solve this challenge by asking the policy maker in charge of the process to share his concept of social capital. There was even a monographic session of the direction board for that. In retrospect, we think that we tried to solve the challenge with a banking approach, when what we needed was a shared unveiling process that would make us conscious of everybody's taken for granted assumptions. We needed awareness.

In the second stage of the project with the new government there was also a clear idea to change the approach to territorial development. But this time the definition of territorial development was undertaken through various workshops and meetings where a wide range of policy makers and researchers contributed with our perspectives. This helped reflect on our roles in the project. The learning process with the first government, though apparently fruitless in the first stage, had been useful as the need for unveiling and awareness had become (without naming them that way) part of our collective knowing in GS.

The case shows that even in approaches where we seemingly work in Mode 2, we might not be approaching problems in depth. Unless we have an adequate approach to the pedagogical process and the construction of awareness, we may keep the cogeneration process on the surface. If we want research to change the attitudes and behaviour of territorial actors, we can hardly rely on a process where researchers create the knowledge first and then transfer it to the actors. Nor can we rely on processes where researchers and practitioners diagnose a problem without unveiling its real nature. Unveiling should generate the awareness of everybody's part in the problem and everybody's contribution to the solution.

Our reflection on the case is that the second stage of the project – by first creating the space for learning and then evolving to policy design and intervention – did not follow the usual pattern. In most projects in which we have worked with policy makers, the process is initiated in the lower circles in Figure 7.1. By the time the decision is made to initiate such processes, somebody (either a researcher or policy maker) has reached conclusions on what the problem is, and others are brought into the project to solve this problem. There is seldom the time and money to initiate a process where all participants' understandings of the problem can be unveiled and the project designed to be significant for all affected, linking the process to their inner schemes so that they all see themselves as part of the process.

ON THE IDEOLOGICAL POSITION OF RESEARCHERS

We will now focus on the case description presented in this chapter, concretely in the moment when the decision was made to move from the space for learning in Figure 7.1 to the one for co-ordination and policy design, trying to design a policy that would create a different approach to territorial development.

Researchers and policy makers discussed Gustavsen's framework for change (presented in Chapter 6). The policy makers' first reaction was that it addressed 'how' the intervention would be developed, but not 'what' they were going to intervene on. The definition of territorial development as a *process* of mobilisation and participation of different actors had emphasised the process perspective and the focus on 'how'. The following is a fragment from the diary in which the discussion was documented:

> GS aims at generating concrete changes, but with the final goal of a change in paradigm and must always introduce in the process this questioning/ reflection about the paradigm. If we have a framework that aims at a change of paradigm through 'how' we intervene but we apply it to the 'what' that has always been the object of intervention in the previous paradigm, are we really approaching a change in paradigm? This means,

if we have an innovative participatory approach, but we apply it to the traditional innovation policy, what kind of change are we generating?
(Gipuzkoa Sarean, 2012b, p. 4)

From that day on this issue was framed in GS as the 'dialogue on change of paradigm' and we were all aware that it had an ideological component. Politicians emphasised their desire to develop this dialogue not just among policy makers, but in every space they met with territorial actors.

They key fact here is that we were aware that 'what' would be linked to the ideological position of the government. But we were also aware that 'how' and 'what' were not independent from each other and we, researchers, were deeply involved in 'how'. Our main argument reflecting on Freire and the case is that our choice to embrace AR in this project is as ideological as the decision of politicians in the project to discuss the change of paradigm.

This drives the discussion to a dimension that is very present in Freire's discourse, but which we have missed in many of the territorial development processes we have been part of: the ideological discussion. We interpret *ideology* as the set of beliefs a group or society uses to render reality intelligible. There is no policy design or intervention that does not respond to a given ideology. It is either implicit or explicit. The same applies to research. There is no methodological approach to research that does not respond to a given ideology. This is a hard affirmation for many researchers.

There is no neutrality. What varies is the degree of awareness participants in a process have of either reinforcing or unveiling an ideological position (Freire, 2008b, p. 17). This is as applicable to researchers participating in the agora as to policy makers, and as applicable to the definition of 'what' policy learning should achieve as to 'how' it should achieve it. This means that researchers, as actors in territorial development, are part of the ideological discussion, and their praxis is inevitably linked to their ideological position.

The ideological discussion on the methodological approaches to research has been absent, or at least not explicit, in the territorial development discourse in terms of the RIS presented in Part I. This does not mean there is no implicit ideological position of the researchers. It probably means that we are taking the position for granted. Without an explicit discourse, the issues related to RISs are apparently approached as a challenge of increasing the technical efficiency of the system. There is no open discourse on the model of society we want to construct through them. This efficiency approach has often led us to follow good practice and copy and paste policies without linking them to all our taken-for-granted beliefs.

Both Bjørn Gustavsen and Paulo Freire approach change beyond the efficiency of the system. They have an idea of the society they want to construct, and they share it with the reader. What is inspiring for us is that they both propose dialogue processes as a way to approach people and interact with them in the pursuit of social change, without exclusively presenting an abstract discussion on it.

REVISITING THE SPACES IN THE AGORA

In order to integrate the previous discussions in our approach to the agora, we will build on Figure 7.1 and reformulate the 'space for learning' as a 'space for awareness', where the ideological dialogue takes place to generate the critical awareness proposed by Freire (see Figure 7.2). This is done by coding and decoding, as a result of the interaction between the abstract and the concrete that gives way to a problem-posing approach. The goal in such a process is to prevent territorial actors (policy makers and researchers included) from being completely sure of their certainties. Following the directions of the author of the original diagram and our later reflections, the three spaces should not be interpreted linearly. That is why we have also changed their position.

In the Introduction to this book we defined the agora as a relational space and, following Murdoch (2006), argued that it is a power-filled space in which some alignments come to dominate, at least for a period, while others come to be dominated. After discussing Freire's approach to ideology, this makes sense in the agora. The space for awareness should be a space where different ideological positions are unveiled and confronted through dialogue. It is the dialogue in the space for awareness that can bring about change in paradigms. Without an explicit ideological dialogue, the phases of policy design and intervention will focus on the efficiency of the system.

The space for awareness must be a space where participants are faced with their own contradictions. In the various processes where we have been inspired by the problem-posing approach proposed by Freire, we have seen how shocking this can be. Researchers and policy makers seldom work in a problem-posing way that makes them see that *they* must change. As researchers, we have heard the criticism that the university and research is not good in a particular territory, that society should be getting more value

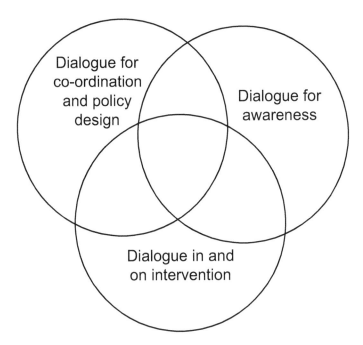

Figure 7.2   **The agora represented as the combination of different spaces for dialogue**

out of it. But seldom have we, as individual researchers, faced the need to take the problem as our own and change. That is what we have found most stimulating in Freire's approach. By sequences of coding and decoding, the problem is posed in a way that creates pressure to change. We have seen that sometimes inertia is so great or situations become so stressful that researchers and/or practitioners prefer to return to banking approaches. But used in this way, the space for awareness is the part of the agora where the conflict we focused on in Chapter 2 can be made explicit, initiating the path to consensus and action.

In this new interpretation in Figure 7.2, the three spaces partly overlap. These are the interactions on the cogenerative processes in the three spaces. The awareness developed impregnates the policy definition and intervention. Praxis in the definition of and intervention in the policy process feeds a new cycle of reflection in the space of awareness. This is how we interpret the action research approach in the democratic agora, where action and reflection are part of one and the same process.

Closing Comments

Throughout this chapter we have reflected on the pedagogical process in agoras in the context of research projects. In this section we will return to the story with which we opened the introduction to this chapter and reflect on other type of agoras that we consider have an understudied potential for territorial development: the formal educational processes fostered by universities.

It would be too wide a discussion for this section to reflect on the whole university system. We propose to think about master's degrees and PhD courses for territorial development, which are designed for practitioners and researchers in this field. And we propose to think about them in terms of Freire's pedagogical approach to designing educational processes.

To do so, we go back to the master's course in territorial development we visited in Rafaela. The following is a fragment of the discussion of the Rafaela case with GS policy makers:

> relevance of training, not only as an element for specialisation, but for the construction of a shared vision of the actors. This need was completely internalised by the territorial actors in Rafaela. It was them who created the Master in territorial development where various actors from different organisations of the territory participate. This has been critical for the construction of a shared language and a shared vision ....
> (minutes from GS meeting, 17 February 2012)

We have seen university training *in company*, demanded by a specific organisation and tailored to their needs. But we seldom find master's and PhD programmes *in territory*. It is hard to find these formal training processes created and designed together with territorial actors. It is usually academia that does so, in a way that is closer to the banking than the problem-posing approach. But what makes it possible to generate educational processes that are linked to the initiative of the territorial actors and at the same time are part of the formal training at a university? We again reflect on the case of Rafaela and what seems to be the origin of their actual approach to education for territorial development:

> Beginning in 1991 ... the team with the highest political responsibility systematically met every Friday afternoon and Saturday morning with

the goal of learning, discussing about politics, look for a shared language and vision, talk and agree on work programmes. It was not only 'the others' that had to train or be educated. There were clear needs of those who had to design and execute public policy. In time, these spaces were used for the coordination among different civil servants, which contributed to the solution of a problem linked to the compartmented essence of public administration .... In a short time every member of the cabinet received, beside this cycle of workshops and training, education outside Argentina. This reinforced not only technical capabilities, but also helped them better approach change processes.

(Costamagna and Larrea, 2011)

There is a 20-year learning process between the initiative of the political team just described and the creation of the master's in territorial development described in the introduction. But they are part of the same process. Throughout that process, many training projects – informal as well as formal – have been developed to support territorial development. There is a common understanding of the role of education in territorial development that is integrated into the shared vision of Rafaela, but also into the routines of participants. It is the construction of this shared vision and patterns of behaviour in the territory, as an ongoing process for decades, that creates the conditions to use formal training programmes at the university as educational contexts with a problem-posing approach. This is, of course, not a recipe for others to follow, but a case for reflection on the under-studied and underestimated role of formal training programmes in universities as agoras for territorial development.

Concluding Reflections: Creating Connectedness

In the Introduction to this book we posed two main challenges. The first was how social researchers can engage with and play a more direct role in territorial development. The second was how policy makers can learn and redefine policy making approaches to territorial development. Throughout the previous seven chapters we have discussed these challenges in the intersection of territorial development and action research. Our main proposal is that researchers and territorial actors must meet in agoras and create collective knowing, which is fundamental for generating actionable knowledge for changes in territories. Collective knowing is knowledge generated in action by actors participating and collaborating to create social innovation in situations of territorial complexity by moving from conflict to consensus. We have argued in favour of a pluralistic action research approach for generating collective knowing.

Our more detailed arguments in the intersection of territorial development and action research have been presented throughout the preceding chapters. There is nothing more we wish to add to the discussion except this question: is the writing of this book enough to contribute to these challenges, or are there any further steps left for us to meet these goals? We answer to this question later in this section of concluding reflections by introducing the concept of *connectivity*.

The decision to write inside out from micro processes did not come solely from the aim of looking at territorial development from a different angle. It was also about creating a book that could help others working in the same intersection. By writing inside out and connecting concrete experiences to new concepts and frameworks, we wanted to make it easier for readers to integrate such concepts and frameworks into their own concrete processes.

These aims are related to what Gustavsen et al. (2007) define as the *challenge of scope*. They argue that after the first experience, we cannot let theory speak alone, because of the abstraction from context. Freire (1996) has a similar approach, in which he describes processes as a continuous movement from the concrete to the abstract, and then back to the concrete.

Validity is the concept that connects with the challenge of scope and helps us to reflect on how the aims of the book could be met. We also include some considerations on how this research can connect to contexts other than those discussed in the different chapters. We will first summarise the main discussions in the book, in order to clarify which concepts and frameworks we have in mind when we reflect on validity. Then we will reflect on the issue of validity before making some final comments.

The Main Discussions in the Book

The main discussions have been grouped into three sections that correspond to the three different parts of the book.

SOCIAL INNOVATION, CONFLICT AND COLLECTIVE KNOWING IN AGORAS FOR TERRITORIAL DEVELOPMENT

Regional innovation systems and the related territorial development literature do not extensively analyse the role of social researchers in territorial development. Practice shows that researchers in this field have often played the role of the outsider without being explicit about this position. This approach sees the social researcher as someone who observes the system from the outside, diagnosing it and giving recommendations to policy makers on how it can improve its efficiency. In Chapter 1 we proposed that there is another role social researchers can play in an effective territorial development process – the generation of social innovation. This is defined as innovation in the way actors relate to each other and can be applied to regional innovation systems. It is the connection between social and technological innovation that leads to territorial development. But social innovation in regional innovation systems has been under-studied and underestimated in terms of its influence on territorial development. Our argument is that social researchers should be more explicit about their position as part of a regional innovation system. The agora is the space where researchers and territorial actors, such as policy makers, can meet and interact in territorial development processes.

In Chapter 2 we introduced the concept of territorial complexity. These are situations where there is a diversity of interdependent but autonomous actors, who may have different perspectives on the issues that affect all of them, but without any of them having a hierarchical position to solve the shared problems by instructing the others on how to proceed. Such a situation requires approaches other than command and obey, which in many cases results in the creation of policy networks as collaborative approaches to development. These are often examples of agoras. But it is not easy to evolve from frameworks based on decision making in hierarchical structures to policy networks. One of the critical elements facing territorial complexity is understanding conflict as a natural situation that must be managed, not avoided. Conflict is sometimes explicit in an agora, but can also be implicit. Consequently, the processes social researchers face in the agora are to a great extent processes for making conflict explicit and constructing consensus for action. This type of process sometimes develops in the formal events designed for the process (onstage), but at other times requires a deep involvement of researchers and practitioners in keeping the dialogue alive even when there is no formal context for it (backstage).

The challenge for the social researcher in the agora is thus to contribute to facing conflict in order to reach action. In Chapter 3 we argued that this has to do with the development of social capital (networks, trust and a shared vision). But social capital is not an aim in itself. It should contribute to collective knowing, a capability shared by the actors in policy networks to cogenerate knowledge in and on action. This will make policy learning in policy networks possible. The interpretation of policy learning exclusively in cognitive terms has sometimes led us (social researchers) to find solutions in theory, then transfer this knowledge in a linear way to actors in territory. This is what we called 'solutions on paper'. This type of solution has very little effect if it is not connected to action and the development of collective knowing. Collective knowing is not about a homogenising process where practitioners understand what the researchers' solution on paper is and apply it. It is not about asking all actors to integrate into one homogeneous perspective. Collective knowing is about understanding diversity and articulating the variety of perspectives that exist in policy networks to generate knowing that can be workable.

A PLURALISTIC APPROACH TO ACTION RESEARCH

Playing the role of social researchers in the agora requires approaches to research that are not mainstream in territorial development research. In Chapter 4 we used the concepts of Mode 1 and Mode 2 to simplify the different approaches. The first is based on the generation of knowledge in disciplinary environments to be later transferred to actors in the territory, and the second is based on the generation of knowledge in a context of application. Mode 2 has been defined mainly in relation to science and technology, and its implications in social sciences have been less studied. Agoras for territorial development fit with the Mode 2 knowledge creation approach.

Our argument is that agoras for territorial development are Mode 2 spaces of knowledge creation for social innovation (and not only for technological innovation), that will solve situations of territorial complexity and conflict.

The cogenerative action research model argues that researchers are outsiders (external change agents) who connect with internal problem owners. Our argument is that the distinctions between outsiders and insiders are less clear-cut than is often assumed when we refer to agoras for territorial development. Insiders and outsiders build trust, they increase interaction and they develop collective knowing, such as how to work together and how to work with social innovation, territorial complexity and conflict. In this process it is not only the problem owners who change, but also the outsiders – the researchers.

The change to collective knowing is a demanding process for a researcher who is used to working in Mode 1 environments and wants to change to Mode 2. This can be difficult to do in the university environment. It is not enough to have researchers who want to work with a Mode 2 approach. The path from Mode 1 to Mode 2 is a path where researchers and practitioners shape each other's perspectives. Consequently, the change process for researchers must happen in a wider inter-organisational change process in which the university, research organisations and territorial development organisations are involved.

In Chapter 5 we looked more closely at the change process of one specific research organisation that aimed to establish an action research environment. The challenge was posed in terms of changing work habits so that the environment not only contained research, action and participation, but was able to connect them in specific development processes. The main issue addressed in this chapter was the creation of pluralistic environments for action research. By this we mean environments where researchers with very different profiles contribute in different ways to the process and action research develops through the way that such contributions are connected in the process. To make them resilient, it is important for these environments to generate self-awareness about the change process.

THE POLITICAL ROLE OF ACTION RESEARCHERS IN CHANGE PROCESSES

What goes on in the agora is dialogue. In Chapter 6 we proposed the democratic dialogue concept as an appropriate approach to the agora. But dialogue is not just talk. Dialogue can be the path to change. The change process begins with changes in patterns of communication. The creation of a shared language is essential to this. If researchers and policy makers communicate differently, this has an impact on what the development process focuses on and how development is planned. This brings a new governance mode to the agora and territorial development processes which can have an impact on concrete policy tools. The change in policy tools again relates to change in patterns of communication generating cyclical processes. In having dialogue and generating change processes in the agora, there is an issue about the status of researchers and policy makers. In the actual systems for funding projects the funds are either assigned to researchers who decide on the projects or come from policy makers who invite researchers into their processes. This makes it difficult to generate equality of status for researchers and practitioners in the agora. The way research is considered in science and technology policy in each territory sets the framework that shapes action research processes for territorial development.

The mutual shaping process in the agora can be understood as a pedagogical process, and this is what we did in Chapter 7. In order to develop change processes, researchers and practitioners must avoid banking approaches. These are approaches where researchers are understood to have knowledge which they must deposit in the practitioners so that the practitioners will take action accordingly. The problem-posing approach we propose for the agora is one where both researchers and policy makers are aware that they need to change. The new cogenerated knowing will change not only territorial development, but also research. A problem-posing approach develops participants' awareness of their role in the change process. This cannot be done without participants (policy makers and researchers) gaining conscious awareness of their ideological position. We understand ideology as the set of beliefs by which a group or society orders reality so as to render it intelligible. Ideology is one of the elements that keep behaviour unchanged even when the discourse on territorial development changes. But we find few agoras developed together by policy makers and researchers which openly address the ideological discussion. That is why we propose that, together with the dialogue on policy design and policy intervention that are more frequently addressed in territorial development agoras, dialogues for awareness should take place in which different ideological positions are discussed and later connected to policy design and intervention.

We summarise some of these discussions in Table 8.1, outlining one core story of each case, which concepts we used to discuss the case, and what new concepts and frameworks we proposed as a result of the discussion. The goal is to have a simplified framework for the following validity discussion.

Table 8.1   Summary of the discussion

Chapter	Core story of the case	Concepts combined with the case*	Contributions from the discussion
1	EG (which worked on social innovation) could not meet the goal of territorial development alone, nor could the Loiola Foundation (which worked on technological innovation); they merged to develop a stronger approach to territorial development	Regional innovation systems Social innovation	The connection between technological and social innovation. The role of the social researcher in social innovation processes
2	How EG and the Loiola Foundation faced conflict and reached consensus for working together	Territorial complexity Conflict and consensus	The transformation from implicit to explicit conflict and the process of reaching explicit consensus
3	In one period of the development of EG there was only consensus on paper, not in action; the transformation to action (to work together) required a continuous reflection process over a long period	Knowledge versus knowing Social capital	Collective knowing
4	The cogenerative model was used by researchers in Orkestra to develop their approach to action research for territorial development, but one of the conflictive discussions was that they were not seen, and they did not see themselves, as outsiders	Mode 1–Mode 2 knowledge production The cogenerative action research model	A revisited cogenerative model, the social researcher as insider to territorial development
5	Departing from an approach to pragmatism, an Orkestra research team developed its own approach that was later called a pluralistic approach to action research	Action Participation Research Pluralism	Pluralistic action research
6	Researchers in Orkestra evolved from mainly facilitating workshops to being integrated into the working environments of policy makers, for instance in GS	Democratic dialogue Language and action	An adaptation of a framework for change in action research from workplace to territorial development
7	In GS, different spaces were created as the process evolved from reflection to intervention in the territory	The educational process Problem-posing method Awareness The neutrality discussion	The definition of different spaces for policy learning in territorial development

*   The concepts of territorial development, action research and the agora were presented in the Introduction.

The Validity Discussion

Both quantitative and qualitative approaches, including action research, must respond to the issue of validity. In the general meaning of the concept, validity is 'something sound' – well-grounded on good principles or evidence and able to withstand criticism or objection (Eikeland, 2006, p. 197). There are three concepts we have used to reflect on validity: workability, credibility and transferability, concepts often used in qualitative research. Departing from reflections on these concepts, we propose the concept of *connectivity*.

WORKABILITY, CREDIBILITY AND TRANSFERABILITY

Workability considers whether the knowledge generated in action research has been useful for the participants (Greenwood and Levin, 2007). This is a criterion based on the philosophy of pragmatism. It rests upon observations and interpretations, with a commitment to act upon the interpretation, to test the knowledge generated in the agora. The key questions for the participants are: Does this knowledge work? Did it help to solve a problem? Or at least, did the action that followed reflection progress the process one small step further?

Credibility is whether research results are believable. Ensuring credibility is one of most important factors in establishing trustworthiness. Credibility is the arguments and the processes necessary for someone to trust research results (Greenwood and Levin, 2007). Greenwood and Levin distinguish between internal and external credibility.

Internal credibility is related to the actors that generated the findings – the participants in the agora. Internal credibility means that the results of research are integrated into the dialogue with the actors to consider whether the results of research are trustworthy from the perspective of the participants in the process. Do they recognise the story they have participated in? Do they see it as a meaningful description? Do they consider that the concepts and frameworks generated from the process helped them to understand their own story better? The theoretical discussion is also a part of the discussion of a case and is based on assumptions which guide the explanation and the conclusion. Having different assumptions, researchers and practitioners may differ on how they interpret what happened. Checking internal credibility is not a one-off event. The absence of internal credibility (when the interpretation of practitioners of what happened and why and how it happened differs from that of researchers) does not necessarily mean the process failed. It can be interpreted as the discovery of different perspectives on an issue that can lead to a shared learning process. It might signal that there are taken-for-granted assumptions that should be discussed and could contribute to solving the problem. That is why the test for internal credibility is not a final step in the process, but one more step in the construction of collective knowing.

External credibility is related to actors who have not participated in the knowledge creation process. How do they judge the story, the result and the concepts? Do they believe it? Is the knowledge convincing (Greenwood and Levin, 2007)? In academia, this is usually done through peer scrutiny of the research project. This is a complex process based on assumptions connected to how knowledge can be constructed according to different paradigms within quantitative and qualitative research.

The question that is left is whether knowledge we have constructed in one context can be transferred to others for practical use. Transferability is the concept that refers to this (Lincoln and Guba, 1985). Lincoln and Guba argue that it is not possible to make precise statements about how results apply to other contexts. What is possible is to specify a working hypothesis together with a description of the time and the context in which it was found to hold. Whether it holds in some other context, or even in the same context at some other time, is an empirical issue (Lincoln and Guba, 1985, p. 316).

Collective knowing cannot be transferred, since it is a part of the context in which the action took place. What can be transferred is the verbal description of the process and the concepts and frameworks. Lincoln and Guba (1985) argue that transferability is the responsibility of the one doing the verbalisation through thick descriptions. It can be enhanced by how well the text is formulated, but the responsibility still ends with the text. They also argue that since the researcher knows only the 'sending context', he or she cannot make transferability inferences. The responsibility for the further 'transfer' of the results to another context lies with the person who finds the knowledge sensible and wants to apply the knowledge in another context (Lincoln and Guba, 1985).

REFLECTIONS ON THE WORKABILITY AND INTERNAL CREDIBILITY OF THE CONCEPTS AND FRAMEWORKS

In this section we share some thoughts about the workability and internal credibility of the concepts presented in Table 8.1. External credibility and transferability cannot be analysed at this stage.

In the case of Orkestra in Chapter 5 and the case of Gipuzkoa Sarean in Chapters 6 and 7, the concepts have been developed in dialogue with the participants, i.e. in action. The concepts have become a natural part of the dialogue. They are used in the dialogue by the participants to question each other's (including the researchers') arguments, they are used to explain a situation and why specific actions are necessary. The concepts' workability has been tested by the participants throughout the processes that are analysed. In the case of Ezagutza Gunea, only the final part of the case overlaps with the writing process in this book. Consequently, most of the reflections are reflections on action, not *in* action. In these cases we have tested internal credibility but not workability.

To validate is to check (Kvale, 1995). In all cases (EG, Orkestra and GS), internal credibility has been checked with the main actors in the case. We have discussed the chapters with all policy makers and researchers who have a recognisable role in the cases. With some of them we carefully went through every single sentence that made reference to them. Others told us that they didn't want to go through the text, they fully trusted us to have been respectful with what happened, but they wanted to discuss our main conclusions. There were elements they proposed that we add to make the cases more understandable, but none of them asked to remove anything we had written. Although most of the concepts and frameworks made sense to them and they found them credible from the perspective of their experience in the cases, there were some elements that did not completely fit for them. We share two challenges for future research that emerged in these discussions in the following paragraphs.

The first challenge is to do with the relationship between social researchers and territorial actors – in this case, policy makers. For policy makers it made sense to discuss the role of social researchers in the policy process, and they accepted the idea of having social researchers as partners in the dialogue processes for territorial development. However, even if this was accepted, the question of whether we were insiders or outsiders to the process remained unanswered. We were asked this question by several participants during the credibility check. What did it mean?

This discussion might initially sound very theoretical, but there was a practical worry behind it. How can we develop a process in which elected politicians work together with researchers, and thus are influenced by them, without researchers gaining too much power and undermining democratic principles?

This was a worry for some of the actors we worked with. One of the politicians defined his relationship with us, researchers, as a 'good-willed fight'. This is a dilemma for which we have no theoretical solutions. Our position is that the dilemma has to be dealt with in every action research process.

This leads us to the first of the challenges for future research. We have made a contribution in the intersection of action research and an approach to territorial development inspired by regional innovation systems. An issue that has strongly emerged in the case discussions is power. RISs follow an approach to territorial development that does not integrate power as a critical element. But power is one of the main issues for other approaches to territorial development, such as the literature on institutions, leadership and governance (Sotarauta, 2009; 2010; 2012). The credibility discussions held with the participants in the cases show the need to integrate this literature into the intersection of action research and territorial development.

The second challenge is to do with the pluralistic approach to action research. This issue emerged in Chapter 5 in the discussion of how action research had developed in Orkestra. Participants clearly distinguished two stages. One was the moment of bringing action research into Orkestra, which was a moment when action research generated a break with other approaches to research. The second was the path to integrating the different perspectives into shared research processes.

Reflecting on the first stage, one of the researchers said that even though it had been hard, proposing the action research approach versus traditional research in the institute had been positive. She said that if action research had not been presented as something substantially different from what was already done, it would not have found a space of its own in Orkestra, and would have been merged with other approaches (see Chapter 5).

The pluralistic approach to action research outlined in Chapter 5 aims to prevent action research becoming something that creates distance from other researchers. At the same time, we find that there are a community of researchers and a corpus of literature that have been critical in our trajectory, and we would not have been able to connect to it unless the authors had framed it as action research and clearly distinguished it from other approaches. The second challenge faced in credibility discussions is how to develop a pluralistic approach while continuing to develop action research as an approach in its own right.

TAKING TRANSFERABILITY FURTHER: THE CHALLENGE OF CONNECTIVITY

We now begin a discussion on transferability that frames our final reflection on the aim of this book and our compromise regarding such an aim.

When approaching the discussion on validity, a four-field table helped to structure our reflection (see Table 8.2). There were two groups with which we wanted to check validity. One was the internal actors – the actors who had participated in the cases. The other group was the external actors – those who had no connection with the cases, such as other researchers and practitioners in territorial development. There were two main questions we wanted to answer: whether the contents of the book made sense to them, and whether they had integrated the concepts, frameworks and cases into their own reflection and action processes.

We (the authors) discussed the concept of external credibility/transferability. Did we agree with the affirmation that our responsibility ends with delivering the text? Without finding it contradictory to the position of Lincoln and Guba (1985) on the responsibility of researchers in terms of transferability, we saw that we had developed another responsibility in terms of applying and integrating the concepts and frameworks into territorial development projects in other contexts. This is not unusual. But the concept of transferability was not enough to reflect on it.

Table 8.2   Validity

	Internal (for participants in the context of application where the concept or framework was developed)	External (for others, either researchers or practitioners, who did not participate in the context of application where the concept or framework was developed)
It makes sense	Internal credibility	External credibility/transferability
It has been applied in reflection processes in concrete actions	Workability	Connectivity

The contents of the book have mostly been integrated into an ongoing process we have called *learning from differences*, inspired by the use of this phrase by Ennals and Gustavsen (1999) and Gustavsen et al. (2007). This process has materialised through agreements between different research and territorial development organisations in Latin America, Norway and the Basque Country. It has been based on researcher mobility, partly in seminars and workshops, and partly in more engaged participation by researchers in action research projects for territorial development in other countries. One of the reactions of practitioners when this happened was described in Chapter 7. They felt it was good to have foreign researchers as outsiders in their projects as they might see things that were taken for granted, not only by themselves and the other territorial actors, but also by the local researchers.

One of our reflections is that pluralistic approaches can contribute to the connection of disciplinary researchers and action researchers in specific contexts, but they are not limited to this. They should also contribute to the connection of different action researchers located in different environments. This can help to generate more capabilities to develop the awareness of participants of their taken-for-granted assumptions. But beyond that, they can generate a greater critical mass of pluralistic action research, to help it find a place of its own in academic communities.

This experience is at the core of our argument for the need to reflect not only in terms of transferability, but also in terms of connectivity. The concept is inspired by the challenge of creating connectedness posed in the book *Creating Connectedness*, which addressed the challenges of the Norwegian Enterprise Development 2000 programme of 1994–2000 (Gustavsen et al., 2001a). The programme was different to the projects we have presented here, but the challenge is the same: how to create connectedness between different contexts.

We define connectivity as a dialogical approach to transferability. This means that the responsibility of the researchers does not end with the publication of the results. The researcher may make a choice to connect with other environments using the concepts, frameworks and cases developed and to enter a dialogue that will enhance the workability of the concepts in the new contexts. This does not mean that the researcher takes responsibility for the new process, but he or she takes responsibility for connecting with its participants (researchers and practitioners) in a dialogue. As it requires the engagement of the researcher, connectivity has a much narrower scope than transferability. Once a research outcome is published, transferability requires no or little further engagement by the researcher. The concepts and frameworks can reach a few or many actors and researchers, but reaching many requires very little additional effort by the author. Connectivity requires the involvement of the researcher/ author in every new context where the concepts and frameworks are integrated into a process. That is why there is a limited scope for connectivity, as there is a limit to the number of new contexts a researcher can interact with. In this sense, we find that transferability and connectivity should be understood in complementary terms. That is our compromise with this book.

Our Hope for the Book

In the Introduction to this book we argued that territorial development is constructed through engagement by the people living and working in the territory. Innovation and territorial development are a result of social processes. On the one hand it is that simple, and on the other hand it is that complex. To deal with complexity, researchers often create new concepts. Some of these concepts are adopted by policy makers and used in policy making processes in their host territories. Often the chosen concepts are the ones that fit best with policy makers' positions, plans and aims. However, if these concepts are not connected to the reality in the territory and to the people living and working there, they will remain solutions on paper, and will fail. Such processes are a waste of time and money, but more importantly, they are a waste of policy makers' and researchers' credibility, and weaken future support for research and policy making processes.

One of the policy makers in Gipuzkoa Sarean addressed this issue. He acknowledged that the shared processes between researchers and practitioners could fail. He argued that in order to preserve this kind of process and obtain the expected results, four conditions needed to be met. The first was a political guarantee that the outcome of the process would be respected. The second was access between those who can decide and those who have the knowledge. This is related to power, as those who can make decisions give up some of their power in favour of a determined process. The third was that, participants, either policy makers or researchers, had to be able to give up personal ambitions to prioritise the project goals. Finally, there had to be a mutual personal admiration[1] between policy makers and researchers – something that goes beyond mere politeness.

---

1   The term 'admiration' has provoked comments when we have shared this text. We have realised that the word 'admiration' is interpreted differently in different countries and contexts. The expression reflects literally what the policy maker said, and 'admiration' was chosen by him to make a clear distinction from mere politeness. This is probably a very context sensitive condition,

Policy making processes are necessary and important for territorial development. In order to improve the way they are implemented, we think more attention should be paid to what we presented as *awareness* in Chapter 7. Our wish and hope for the future is that awareness will become a part of policy making processes. This is the way to proceed if we accept the fact that contexts differ so much from territory to territory that one-size-fits-all strategies do not work. The answer has to be created each time in each territory. This is the uniqueness of social processes, and it is the uniqueness of innovation. Even if a process has been a success in a neighbouring territory, it is not enough to copy and paste and implement it. Solutions need to be created with the people in the territory through a social process which is a unique social process for the participants in that specific process. This is what makes awareness essential. Unless and until this simple fact is acknowledged, new concepts will only create ripples on the surface.

Action research can contribute to bringing awareness into policy making processes. This is an initial step in the process of creating collective knowing. That is why we believe that there is a need for a field of *action research in territorial development* that builds on both action research and territorial development, but with distinct features at the intersection.

The basis for this field is a continuous dialogue between theory and practice – reflection and action, researchers and practitioners – in the agoras for territorial development. Continuous discussion and mutual shaping of theory and practice bring a continuously renewed interpretation of concepts and frameworks. The interpretation of many of the concepts will vary between one agora and another. Our hope is that the discussions presented in this book will support you, the reader of this book, in new processes in agoras, and that they will help you, together with other actors, to gain awareness of the situation. We hope this will lead to a process of creation and re-creation of the concepts until they are meaningful enough to transform the agoras. That is why we will close with a statement that, despite being a cliché, represents our wish for this book.

We hope that the moment when you finish reading this book is not an ending, but a new beginning.

---

but often this is the glue that makes the process continue despite power play, conflict and hard discussions.

References

Alburquerque, F. (2000) *Manual del Agente de Desarrollo Local*. Santiago de Chile: Ediciones Sur.

Alburquerque, F. (2012) 'Desarrollo Territorial'. In: Orkestra (ed.) *Gipuzkoa Sarean Working Document*. Donostia/San Sebastián: Orkestra.

Alburquerque, F., Costamagna, P. and Ferraro, C. (2008) *Desarrollo Local, Descentralización y Democracia. Ideas Para Un Cambio*. Buenos Aires: UNSAM EDITA.

Aranguren, M.J. and Larrea, M. (2011) 'Regional Innovation Policy Processes: Linking Learning to Action'. *Journal of the Knowledge Economy* 2: 569–85.

Aranguren, M.J., Larrea, M. and Mujika, A. (2007) *Las Empresas Pequeñas del Urola Medio: Bases para la Competitividad*. Azkoitia: Iraurgi Lantzen.

Aranguren, M.J., Larrea, M. and Wilson, J.R. (2010a) 'Learning from the Local: Governance of Networks for Innovation in the Basque Country'. *European Planning Studies* 18: 47–66.

Aranguren, M.J., Larrea, M. and Wilson, J.R. (2010b) 'Trayectorias de Cambio en la Gobernanza: Experiencias en Asociaciones Clúster y Redes comarcales en el País Vasco'. *Ekonomiaz* 74: 160–77.

Aranguren, M.J., Karlsen, J. and Larrea, M. (2012a) 'Regional Collaboration: The Glue that Makes Innovation Happen?' In: Johnsen, H.C.G. and Ennals, R. (eds) *Creating Collaborative Advantage: Innovation and Knowledge Creation in Regional Economies*. Farnham: Gower, pp. 113–22.

Aranguren, M.J., Larrea, M. and Wilson, J.R. (2012b) 'Academia and Public Policy: Towards the Co-generation of Knowledge and Learning Processes'. In: Asheim, B. and Parrilli, M.D. (eds) *Interactive Learning for Innovation: A Key Driver for Clusters and Innovation Systems*. Basingstoke: Palgrave Macmillan, pp. 275–89.

Argyris, C. and Schön, D.A. (1974) *Theory in Practice: Increasing Professional Effectiveness,* San Francisco, CA: Jossey-Bass.

Argyris, C. and Schön, D.A. (1991) 'Participatory Action Research and Action Science Compared: A Commentary'. In: Whyte, W.F. (ed.) *Participatory Action Research*. Newbury: Sage.

Argyris, C. and Schön, D.A. (1996) *Organizational Learning II: Theory, Method, and Practice*. Reading, MA: Addison-Wesley.

Asheim, B. (1996) 'Industrial Districts as "Learning Regions": A Condition for Prosperity?' *European Planning Studies* 4: 379–400.

Asheim, B. (2001) 'Learning Regions as Development Coalitions: Partnership as Governance in European Workfare States?' *Concepts and Transformation. International Journal of Action Research and Organizational Renewal* 6: 73–101.

Asheim, B. (2011) 'Strong Research and Innovation Milieus: A New Regional Innovation Policy?' In: Johnsen, H.C.G. and Pålshaugen, Ø. (eds) *Hva er innovasjon? Perspektiver i norsk innovasjonsforskning Bind I: System og innovasjon*. Kristiansand: Høyskoleforlaget, pp. 97–126.

Asheim, B. and Coenen, L. (2006) 'Contextualising Regional Innovation Systems in a Globalising Learning Economy: On Knowledge Bases and Institutional Frameworks'. *Journal of Technology Transfer* 31: 163–73.

Asheim, B. and Gertler, M. (2005) 'The Geography of Innovation: Regional Innovation Systems'. In: Fagerberg, J., Mowery, D. and Nelson, R. (eds) *The Oxford Handbook of Innovation*. Oxford: Oxford University Press, pp. 291–317.

Asheim, B. and Hansen, H.K. (2009) 'Knowledge Bases, Talents, and Contexts: On the Usefulness of the Creative Class Approach in Sweden'. *Economic Geography* 85: 425–42.

Asheim, B. and Isaksen, A. (2002) 'Regional Innovation Systems: The Integration of Local "Sticky" and Global "Ubiquitous" Knowledge'. *Journal of Technology Transfer* 22: 77–86.

Asheim, B.T., Isaksen, A., Nauwelaers, C. et al. (2003) *Regional Innovation Policy for Small–medium Enterprises*. Cheltenham: Edward Elgar.

Asheim, B.T., Coenen, L., Moodysson, J. et al. (2007) 'Constructing Knowledge-based Regional Advantage: Implications for Regional Innovation Policy'. *International Journal of Entrepreneurship and Innovation Management* 7: 140–55.

Asheim, B., Boschma, R. and Cooke, P. (2011a) 'Constructing Regional Advantage: Platform Policies Based on Related Variety and Differentiated Knowledge Bases'. *Regional Studies* 45: 893–904.

Asheim, B.T., Smith, H.L. and Oughton, C. (2011b) 'Regional Innovation Systems: Theory, Empirics and Policy'. *Regional Studies* 45: 875–91.

Barandiaran, X. and Korta, K. (2011) *Social Capital and Values in Gipuzkoa: Assessment and Strategic Directions*. Gipuzkoa: Provincial Council of Gipuzkoa.

Becattini, G. (1979) 'Dal Settore Industrial al Distreto Industriale. Alcune Considerazioni Sull'unitá di Indagine dell'economia Industriale'. *Rivista di Economia e Politica Industriale* Anno V.

Bell, D. (1974) *The Coming of Post-industrial Society: A Venture in Social Forecasting*. London: Heinemann.

Bennett, C.J. and Howlett, M. (1992) 'The Lessons of Learning: Reconciling Theories of Policy Learning and Policy Change'. *Policy Sciences* 25: 275–94.

Berger, P. and Luckmann, T. (1966) *The Social Construction of Reality: A Treatise in the Sociology of Knowledge*. Harmondsworth: Penguin.

Bjørndal, C.R.P. (2004) 'Refleksivitet omkring aksjonsforskerens påvirkning: Fra salmer til jazz i kjøkkenet'. In: Tiller, T. (ed.) *Aksjonsforskning – i skole og utdanning*. Kristiansand: Høyskoleforlaget.

Boschma, R.A. and Iammarino, S. (2009) 'Related Variety, Trade Linkages and Regional Growth in Italy'. *Economic Geography* 85: 289–311.

Bourdieu P. (1986) 'The Forms of Capital'. In: Richardson, J.G. (ed.) *Handbook of Theory and Research for the Sociology of Education*. New York: Greenwood, pp. 241–58.

Brown, J.S. and Duguid, P. (1991) 'Organizational Learning and Communities-of-practice: Toward a Unified View of Working, Learning and Innovation'. *Organization Science* 2: 40–57.

Brunsson, N. (2007) 'Organized Hypocrisy'. In: Brunsson, N. (ed.) *The Consequences of Decision-making*. Oxford: Oxford University Press.

Castells, M. (2000) *The Rise of the Network Society*. Oxford: Blackwell

Chatterton, P. and Goddard, J. (2000) 'The Response of Higher Education Institutions to Regional Needs'. *European Journal of Education* 35: 475–96.

Chombart de Lauwe, P.H. (1976) 'Appropriation de l'espace et Changement Social'. In: Korosec-Serfaty, P. (ed.) *Appropriation de l'espace* (minutes from the 3rd IAPS Conference). Strasbourg: Université Louis Pasteur, and CIACO, Université de Louvain-la-Neuve.

Chomsky, N. (1966) *Cartesian Linguistics*. New York: Harper & Row.

Chomsky, N. (2010) 'Some Simple Evo-devo Theses: How True Might They be for Language?' In: Larson, R.K., Deprez, V.M. and Yamakido, H. (eds) *Approaches to the Evolution of Language*. Cambridge: Cambridge University Press.

Cicourel, A.V. (1973) *Cognitive Sociology*. Harmondsworth: Penguin.

Cooke, P. (1992) 'Regional Innovation Systems: Competitive Regulation in the New Europe'. *Geoforum* 23: 365–82.

Cooke, P. (1998) 'Introduction: Origins of the Concept'. In: Braczyk, H.-J., Cooke, P. and Heidenreich, M. (eds) *Regional Innovation Systems*. London: UCL Press, pp. 2–25.

Cooke, P. and Leydesdorff, L. (2006) 'Regional Development in the Knowledge-based Economy: The Construction of Advantage. Introduction to Special Issue'. *Journal of Technology Transfer* 31: 5–15.

Cooke, P., Boekholt, P. and Tödtling, F. (2000) *The Governance of Innovation in Europe. Regional Perspectives on Global Competitiveness*. London: Pinter.

Cooke, P., Laurentis, C., Tödtling, F. et al. (2007) *Regional Knowledge Economies. Markets, Clusters and Innovation*. Cheltenham: Edward Elgar.

Costamagna, P. (2006) *Políticas e Instituciones para el Desarrollo Territorial*. Santiago de Chile: CEPAL-ILPES-GTZ.

Costamagna, P. and Larrea, M. (2011) 'El Caso Rafaela 1991–1995: Los Primeros Años de una Experiencia de Largo Plazo. Reflexiones Para Gipuzkoa Sarean'. Internal project document. Donostia/San Sebastián: Orkestra.

Costamagna, P. and Saltarelli, N. (2004) 'Las Agencias de Desarrollo Local como Promotoras de la Competitiviad de las Pyme'. In: Rhi Sausi, J.L. (ed.) *Desarrollo Local en América Latina. Logros y Desafíos Para la Cooperación Europea*. Caracas: CeSPI Nueva Sociedad.

De Bruijn, P. and Lagendijk, A. (2005) 'Regional Innovation Systems in the Lisbon Strategy'. *European Planning Studies* 13: 1,153–72.

Dewey, J. (1916) *Democracy and Education: An Introduction to the Philosophy of Education*. New York: Macmillan.

Dewey, J. (1923) 'The School as a Means of Developing a Social Consciousness and Social Ideals in Children'. *Journal of Social Forces* 1: 513–17.

Dewey, J. and Bentley, A.F. (1975) *Knowing and the Known*. Westport, CT: Greenwood Press.

Edquist, C. (1997) *Systems of Innovation: Technologies, Institutions and Organizations*. London: Pinter.

Edquist, C. (2005) 'Systems of Innovation: Perspectives and Challenges'. In: Fagerberg, J., Mowery, D. and Nelson, R. (eds) *The Oxford Handbook of Innovation*. Oxford: Oxford University Press, pp. 181–208.

Eikeland, O. (2006) 'Validity in Action Research – Validity of Action Research'. In: Aagard Nielsen, K. and Svensson, L. (eds) *Beyond Practice and Theory*. Maastrict: Shaker Verlag, 193–240.

Emery, F.E. and Thorsrud, E. (1969) *Form and Content in Industrial Democracy*. London: Tavistock Publications.

Emery, F.E. and Thorsrud, E. (1976) *Democracy at Work: The Report of the Norwegian Industrial Democracy Program*. Leiden: Martinus Nijhoff Social Sciences Division.

Ennals, R. and Gustavsen, B. (1999) *Work Organization and Europe as a Development Coalition*. Amsterdam: John Benjamins.

Estensoro, M. (2012) *Local Networks and Socially Innovative Territories: The Case of the Basque Region and Goierri County*. Bilbao: University of the Basque Country.

Estensoro, M. and Larrea, M. (2012) 'The Evolution of Local Development Agencies from Service Providers to Facilitators in Knowledge Networks in the Basque Country: The Role of Academic Expertise in the Change Process'. In: Bellini, N., Danson, M. and Halkier, H. (eds) *Regional Development Agencies: The Next Generation?* London: Routledge.

Etzkowitz, H. and Leydesdorff, L. (2001) *Universities and the Global Knowledge Economy: A Triple Helix of University–Industry–Government Relations.* London and New York: Continuum.

European Commission (2006) *Constructing Regional Advantage: Principles – Perspectives – Policies.* Final Report. Brussels: DG Research.

European Commission (2012) *Guide to Research and Innovation Strategies for Smart Specialisations* (RIS 3). Brussels: European Commission.

Farr, J. (2004) 'Social Capital: A Conceptual History'. *Political Theory* 32: 6–33.

Farr, J. (2007) 'In Search of Social Capital'. *Political Theory* 35: 54–61.

Fine, B. (2007) 'Eleven Hypotheses on the Conceptual History of Social Capital'. *Political Theory* 35: 47–53.

Fine, B. (2010) *Theories of Social Capital: Researchers Behaving Badly.* London: Pluto Press.

Foray, D. (2009) 'Understanding "Smart Specialisation"'. In: Pontikakis, D., Kyriakou, D. and van Bavel, R. (eds) *The Questions of R&D Specialisation: Perspectives and Policy Implications.* Luxembourg: Office for Official Publications of the European Communities.

Foray, D., David, P.A. and Hall, B.H. (2009) *Smart Specialisation: The Concept.* Knowledge Economists Policy Brief 9. Brussels: European Commission.

Foray, D., David, P.A. and Hall, B.H. (2011) *Smart Specialization: From Academic Idea to Political Instrument, the Surprising Career of a Concept and the Difficulties Involved in its Implementation.* MTEI Working Paper 2011-001. Lausanne: Management of Technology & Entrepreneurship Institute, College of Management of Technology, École polytechnique fédérale de Lausanne.

Freire, P. (1996) *Pedagogy of the Oppressed.* Harmondsworth: Penguin Books.

Freire P. (2008a) *Pedagogía de la Autonomía. Saberes Necesarios para la Práctica Educativa.* Buenos Aires: Siglo XXI.

Freire, P. (2008b) *Pedagogía de la Esperanza. Un Reencuentro Con la Pedagogía del Oprimido.* Buenos Aires: Siglo XXI.

Gertler, M. (2004) *Manufacturing Culture: The Institutional Geography of Industrial Practice.* Oxford: Oxford University Press.

Gibbons, M., Limoges, C. and Nowotny, H. et al. (1994) *The New Production of Knowledge: The Dynamics of Science and Research in Contemporary Societies.* London: Sage.

Gipuzkoa Sarean (2009) 'Strategy'. Internal report. San Sebastián: Gipuzkoa Sarean.

Gipuzkoa Sarean (2012a) 'Documento de Estrategia 1: Noviembre 2011–Julio 2012'. Working document. San Sebastián: Gipuzkoa Sarean.

Gipuzkoa Sarean (2012b) 'Intervention Strategy'. Working document. San Sebastián: Gipuzkoa Sarean.

Greenwood, D. and Levin, M. (2005) 'Reform of the Social Sciences and of Universities through Action Research'. In: Denzin, N.K. and Lincoln, Y.S. (eds) *Qualitative Research*, 3rd edn. Thousand Oaks, CA: Sage, 43–64.

Greenwood, D. and Levin, M. (2007) *Introduction to Action Research*, 2nd edn. Thousand Oaks, CA: Sage.

Gustavsen, B. (1992) *Dialogue and Development: Theory of Communication, Action Research and the Restructuring of Working Life*. Assen: Van Gorcum.

Gustavsen, B. (2001a) 'Research and the Challenges of Working Life'. In: Gustavsen, B., Finne, H. and Oscarsson, B. (eds) *Creating Connectedness: The Role of Social Research in Innovation Policy*. Amsterdam: John Benjamins, pp. 85–100.

Gustavsen, B. (2001b) 'Theory and Practice: The Mediating Discourse'. In: Reason, P. and Bradbury, H. (eds) *The Handbook of Action Research*. Thousand Oaks, CA: Sage, pp. 17–26.

Gustavsen, B. (2003) 'New Forms of Knowledge Production and the Role of Action Research'. *Action Research* 1: 153–64.

Gustavsen, B. (2008) 'Action Research, Practical Challenges and the Formation of Theory'. *Action Research* 6: 421–37.

Gustavsen, B. (2011) Innovation, Participation and "Constructivist Society"'. In: Ekman, M., Gustavsen, B., Asheim, B. and Pålshaugen, Ø. (eds) *Learning Regional Innovation: Scandinavian Models*. Basingstoke: Palgrave Macmillan.

Gustavsen, B., Finne, H. and Oscarsson, B. (2001) *Creating Connectedness: The Role of Social Research in Innovation Policy*. Amsterdam: John Benjamins.

Gustavsen, B., Nyhan, B. and Ennals, R. (2007) *Learning Together for Local Innovation: Promoting Learning Regions*. Luxembourg: European Centre for the Development of Vocational Training.

Hammersley, M. (1995) *What's Wrong with Ethnography? Methodological Explanations* London: Routledge.

Herr, K. and Anderson, G.L. (2005) *The Action Research Dissertation: A Guide for Students and Faculty*. Thousand Oaks, CA: Sage.

Isaksen, A. (2001) 'Building Regional Innovation Systems: Is Endogenous Industrial Development Possible in the Global Economy?' *Canadian Journal of Regional Science* 1: 101–20.

Isaksen, A. (2007) Clusters, Innovation and the Local Learning Paradox. *International Journal of Entrepreneurship and Innovation Management* (special issue on regional innovation system and innovation clusters) 7: 366–84.

Isaksen, A. (2009) 'The Innovation Dynamics of Global Competitive Regional Clusters: The Case of the Norwegian Centres of Expertise'. *Regional Studies* 43: 1,155–66.

Isaksen, A. and Kalsaas, B.T. (2009) 'Suppliers and Strategies for Upgrading in Global Production Networks: The Case of a Supplier to the Global Automative Industry in a High-cost Location'. *European Planning Studies* 17: 569–85.

Isaksen, A. and Karlsen, J. (2010) 'Different Modes of Innovation and the Challenge of Connecting Universities and Industry: Case Studies of Two Regional Industries in Norway'. *European Planning Studies* 18: 1,993–2,008.

Isaksen, A. and Karlsen, J. (2012a) 'Combined and Complex Mode of Innovation in Regional Cluster Development: Analysis of the Light-weight Material Cluster in Raufoss'. In: Asheim, B. and Parrilli, M.D. (eds) *Interactive Learning for Innovation: A Key Driver within Clusters and Innovation Systems*. Basingstoke: Palgrave Macmillan, pp. 115–35.

Isaksen, A. and Karlsen, J. (2012b) 'What is Regional in Regional Clusters? The Case of the Globally Oriented Oil and Gas Cluster in Agder, Norway'. *Industry and Innovation* 19: 249–63.

Isaksen, A. and Karlsen, J. (2013) 'Can Small Regions Construct Regional Advantages? The Case of Four Norwegian Regions'. *European Urban and Regional Studies*: 243–57.

Iturrioz, C., Aranguren, M.J. and Aragon, C. (2006) '¿La Política Industrial de Cluster/Redes Mejora Realmente la Competitividad Empresarial? Resultados de la Evaluación de Dos Experiencias en la CAPV'. *Ekonomiaz* 60.

James, W. (1978) *Pragmatism and the Meaning of Truth*. Cambridge, MA: Harvard University Press.

Jensen, M.B., Johnson, B., Lorenz, E. et al. (2007) 'Forms of Knowledge and Modes of Innovation'. *Research Policy* 36: 680–93.

Johnsen, H.C.G. (2001) 'Involvement at Work: A Study of Communicative Processes and Individual Involvement in Organizational Development'. *Handelshøjskolen i København, Det økonomiske fakultet*. Copenhagen: Handelshøjskolen i København.

Johnsen, H.C.G. and Normann, R. (2004) 'When Research and Practice Collide: The Role of Action Research When There is a Conflict of Interest with Stakeholders'. *Systemic Practice and Action Research* 17: 207–35.

Johnson, B. (1992) 'Institutional Learning'. In: Lundvall, B.-Å. (ed.) *National Systems of Innovation. Towards a Theory of Innovation and Interactive Learning*. London: Pinter, pp. 23–44.

Karlsen, J. (2007) *The Regional Role of the University: A Study of Knowledge Creation in the Agora between Agder University College and Regional Actors in Agder*.

Theses at NTNU 2007:91. Trondheim: Norwegian University of Science and Technology.

Karlsen, J. (2010) 'Regional Complexity and the Need for Engaged Governance'. *Ekonomiaz* 74: 91–111.

Karlsen, J. and Larrea, M. (2012) 'Emergence of Shared Leadership in the Basque Country'. In: Sotarauta, M., Horlings, I. and Liddle, J. (eds) *Leadership and Change in Sustainable Regional Development*. London: Routledge, pp. 212–33.

Karlsen, J., Isaksen, A. and Spilling, O.R. (2011) 'The Challenge of Constructing Regional Advantages in Peripheral Areas: The Case of Marine Biotechnology in Tromsø, Norway'. *Entrepreneurship & Regional Development* 23: 235–57.

Karlsen, J., Larrea, M., Aranguren, M.J. et al. (2012) 'Bridging the Gap between Academic Research and Regional Development: A Case Study of Knowledge Cogeneration Processes in the Basque Country'. *European Journal of Education* 47: 122–38.

Kaufmann, A. and Tödtling, F. (2000) 'Systems of Innovation in Traditional Industrial Regions: The Case of Styria in a Comparative Perspective'. *Regional Studies* 34: 29–40.

Kickert, W.J.M., Klijn, E.-H. and Koppenjan, J.F. (1997) 'Introduction: A Management Perspective on Policy Networks'. In: Kickert. W.J.M., Klijn, E.-H. and Koppenjan, J.F. (eds) *Managing Complex Networks: Strategies for the Public Sector*. Thousand Oaks, CA: Sage, pp. 1–13.

Kilpinen, E. (2003) 'Clarence Ayres Memorial Lecture: Does Pragmatism Imply Institutionalism?' *Journal of Economic Issues* XXXVII: 291–304.

Kilpinen, E. (2009) 'Pragmatism as a Philosophy of Action'. Paper presented at The First Nordic Pragmatism Conference, Helsinki, Finland, June 2008.

Klev, R. and Levin, M. (2012) *Participative Transformation: Learning and Development in Practising Change*. Farnham: Gower.

Klijn, E.-H. (1997) 'Policy Networks and Network Management: A State of the Art'. In: Kickert, W.J.M., Klijn, E.-H. and Koppenjan, J.F. (eds) *Managing Complex Networks: Strategies for the Public Sector*. London: Sage, pp. 14–34.

Koppenjan, J.F.M. (2007) 'Consensus and Conflict in Policy Networks: Too Much or Too Little?' In: Torfing, J. and Sørensen, E. (eds) *Theories of Democratic Network Governance*. Basingstoke: Palgrave Macmillan, pp. 132–52.

Koppenjan, J.F.M. and Klijn, E.-H. (2004) *Managing Uncertainties in Networks*. London: Routledge.

Kvale, S. (1995) 'The Social Construction of Validity'. *Qualitative Inquiry* 1: 19–40.

Lagendijk, A. (2006) 'Learning from Conceptual Flows in Regional Studies'. *Regional Studies* 40: 385–99.

Larrea, M. (1999) 'Evolución de las Economías de Localización de los Sistemas Productivos Locales de la CAPV'. In: *Tablas Input–output de la Comunidad Autónoma de Euskadi, Análisis de resultados*. San Sebastián: Eustat.

Larrea, M. (2000a) 'Competitividad y Empleo en los Sistemas Productivos Locales de la CAPV'. *Ekonomiaz* 44.

Larrea, M. (2000b) *Sistemas Productivos Locales en la C.A. del País Vasco*. Vitoria: Servicio Central de Publicaciones del Gobierno Vasco.

Larrea, M. (2000c) 'Una Tipología de Sistemas Productivos Locales de la CAPV'. *Estudios Empresariales* 100.

Larrea, M. (2003) 'Clustres y Territorio: Retos del Desarrollo Local en la Comunidad Autónoma del País Vasco'. *Ekonomiaz* 53: 138–59.

Larrea, M., Aranguren, M.J. and Parrilli, M.D. (2007) 'El Papel de Los Procesos de Aprendizaje Comarcales en las Políticas Regionales de Competitividad e Innovación'. In: Mujika, A. (ed.) *Regiones de Conocimiento*. San Sebastián: Universidad de Deusto.

Larrea, M., Mujika, A. and Aranguren, M.J. (2010) 'Access of Small Firms to Knowledge Networks as a Determinant of Local Economic Development'. In: Lenihan, H., Andreosso-O'Callaghan, B. and Hart, M. (eds) *SMEs in a Globalised World: Survival and Growth Strategies on Europe's Geographical Periphery.* Cheltenham: Edward Elgar, pp. 47–66.

Larrea, M., Aranguren, M.J. and Karlsen, J. (2012) 'The Policy Process in Regional Innovation Systems: Targeting Behavioural Value Added of Policy in Gipuzkoa, Basque Country'. In: Cooke, P. and Parrilli, M.D. (eds) *Perspectives on Global and Territorial Change.* London: Palgrave, pp. 150–65.

Ledford, G.E. and Susan, A.M. (1993) 'Looking Backward and Forward at Action Research'. *Human Relations* 46: 1,349–59.

Levin, M. (2007) 'Knowledge and Technology Transfer: Can Universities Promote Regional Development?' In: Burtscher, C., Harding, A., Laske, S. and Scott, A. (eds) *Knowledge Factories: Universities and Territorial Development in the Global Information Age.* Munich: Hampp-Verlag, pp. 39–51.

Lewin, K. (1943) 'Forces Behind Food Habits and Methods of Change'. *Bulletin of the National Research Council*: 35–65.

Lewin, K. (1948) *Resolving Social Conflicts*. New York: Harper.

Lincoln, Y.S. and Guba, E.G. (1985) *Naturalistic Inquiry*. Beverly Hills, CA: Sage.

Lorentzen, A. (2008) 'The Scales of Innovation Spaces'. In: Querejeta, M.J.A., Landart, C.I. and Wilson, R.J. (eds) *Networks, Governance and Economic Development: Bridging Disciplinary Frontiers.* Cheltenham: Edward Elgar, pp. 40–56.

Lundvall, B.-Å. (1988) 'Innovation as an Interactive Process: From User–producer Interaction to the National System of Innovation'. In: Dosi, G., Freeman, C., Silverberg, G. and Soete, L. (eds) *Technical Change and Economic Theory.* London: Frances Pinter.

Lundvall, B.-Å. (1992) *National Systems of Innovation: Towards a Theory of Innovation and Interactive Learning.* London: Pinter.

Lundvall, B.-Å. (2007) 'National Innovation Systems: Analytical Concept and Development Tool'. *Industry & Innovation* 14: 95–119.

Lundvall, B.-Å. and Johnson, B. (1994) 'The Learning Economy'. *Journal of Industry Studies* 1: 23–42.

Marshall, A. (1890) *Principles of Economics*. London: Macmillan.

Marshall, J. (2008) 'Finding Form in Writing for Action Research'. In: Reason, P. and Bradbury, H. (eds) *The Sage Handbook of Action Research, Participatory Inquiry and Practice*. Thousand Oaks, CA: Sage, pp. 682–94.

Martin, R. and Sunley, P. (2003) 'Deconstructing Clusters: Chaotic Concept or Policy Panacea?' *Journal of Economic Geography* 3: 5–35.

Martinsen, V. (2011) *Filosofi: En innføring*, 3rd edn (e-book). Available at: http://www.lulu.com/gb/en/shop/vegard-martinsen/filosofi-en-innf% C3%B8ring/ebook/product-17357092.html (accessed 28 October 2013).

Metcalfe, J.S. (1994) 'Evolutionary Economics and Technology Policy'. *The Economic Journal* 104: 931–94.

Moulaert, F. and Nussbaumer, J. (2005) 'The Social Region: Beyond the Territorial Dynamics of the Learning Economy'. *Urban and Regional Studies* 12: 45–64.

Murdoch, J. (2006) *Post-structuralist Geography*. Thousand Oaks, CA: Sage.

Nahapiet, J. and Ghoshal, S. (1998) 'Social Capital, Intellectual Capital, and the Organizational Advantage'. *The Academy of Management Review* 23: 242–66.

Nauwelaers, C. and Wintjes, R. (2008) 'Innovation in Policy: Policy Learning within and across Systems and Clusters'. In: Nauwelaers, C. and Wintjes, R. (eds) *Innovation Policy in Europe: Measurement and Strategy*. Cheltenham: Edward Elgar, pp. 225–68.

Navarro, M. and Larrea, M. (2007) *Indicadores y Análisis de Competitividad Local en El País Vasco*. Vitoria-Gasteiz: Servicio Central de Publicaciones del Gobierno Vasco.

Navarro, M. and Magro, E. (2013) *Complejidad y Coordinación en las Estrategias Territoriales: Reflexiones desde el Caso Vasco*. Bilbao: Ekonomiaz.

Nelson, R. and Winter, S.G. (1982) *An Evolutionary Theory of Economic Change*. Cambridge, MA: Belknap Press of Harvard University Press.

Niosi, J., Saviotti, P., Bellon, B. et al. (1993) 'National Systems of Innovation: In Search of Workable Concepts'. *Technology in Society* 15: 207–27.

Nowotny, H., Scott, P. and Gibbons, M. (2001) *Re-thinking Science: Knowledge and the Public in an Age of Uncertainty*. Cambridge: Polity Press.

OECD (2011) 'Higher Education Institutes (HEIs)'. *Innovation Policy Platform*. Paris: OECD.

Olson, M. (1965) *The Logic of Collective Action: Public Goods and the Theory of Groups*. Cambridge, MA: Harvard University Press.

Orkestra (2008) *Presentation of Results of the First DEPURE Subproject*. Strasbourg: Interreg III C Program.

Orlikowski, W.J. (2002) 'Knowing in Practice: Enacting a Collective Capability in Distributed Organizing'. *Organization Science* 13: 249–73.

Ostrom, E. (1990) *Governing the Commons: The Evolution of Institutions for Collective Action*. Cambridge: Cambridge University Press.

Pålshaugen, Ø. (2004) 'How to Do Things with Words: Towards a Linguistic Turn in Action Research?' *Concepts and Transformation: International Journal of Action Research and Organizational Renewal* 9: 181–203.

Pålshaugen, Ø. (2007) 'On the Diversity of Action Research'. *International Journal of Action Research* 3: 9–14.

Pålshaugen, Ø. (2013) 'Meta-theory and Practice: A Plea for Pluralism in Innovation Studies'. In: Johnsen, H.C.G. and Pålshaugen, P. (eds) *Hva er innovasjon? Perspektiver i norsk innovasjonsforskning*. Oslo: Cappelen Damm Akademisk, pp. 286–306.

Parrilli, M.D., Aranguren, M.J. and Larrea, M. (2010) 'The Role of Interactive Learning to Close the "Innovation Gap" in SME Based Local Economies: A Furniture Cluster in the Basque Country and its Key Policy Implications'. *European Planning Studies* 18: 351–70.

Pearce, C.L. and Conger, J.A. (2003) 'All Those Years Ago: The Historical Underpinnings of Shared Leadership'. In: Pearce, C.L. and Conger, J.A. (eds) *Shared Leadership: Reframing the Hows and Whys of Leadership*. Thousand Oaks, CA: Sage, pp. 1–18.

Peirce, C.S. (1905) 'What Pragmatism Is'. *The Monist* 15: 161–81.

Peirce, C.S. (1931–58) *The Collected Papers of Charles Sanders Peirce, Volume V: Pragmatism and Pragmaticism*. Cambridge, MA: Harvard University Press.

Pettigrew, P.J. (2003) 'Power, Conflicts, and Resolutions: A Change Agent's Perspective on Conducting Action Research within a Multiorganizational Partnership'. *Systemic Practice and Action Research* 16: 375–91.

Pinheiro, R., Benneworth, P. and Jones, G.A. (2012) 'Understanding Regions and the Institutionalization of Universities'. In: Pinheiro, R., Benneworth, P. and Jones, G.A. (eds) *Universities and Regional Development*. Abingdon: Routledge, pp. 11–32.

Polanyi, M. (1966) *The Tacit Dimension*. New York: Doubleday.

Porter, M.E. (1990) *The Competitive Advantage of Nations*. New York: Free Press.

Porter, M.E. (1998) *On Competition*. Boston, MA: Harvard Business School Press.

Powell, W. (1990) 'Neither Market Nor Hierarchy: Network Forms of Organization'. *Research in Organizational Behavior* 12: 295–336.

Putnam, R.D. (1995) 'Tuning In, Tuning Out: The Strange Disappearance of Social Capital in America'. *Political Science & Politics* 28: 664–83.

Readings, B. (1996) *The University in Ruins*. Cambridge, MA: Harvard University Press.

Reason, P. and Bradbury, H. (2001) *Handbook of Action Research: Participative Inquiry and Practice*. London: Sage.

Reason, P. and Bradbury, H. (2008) *The Sage Handbook of Action Research Participative Inquiry and Practice*. London: Sage.

Rørvik, K.A. (2007) *Trender og translasjoner: Ideer som former det 21. århundrets organisasjon*. Oslo: Universitetsforlaget.

Ryle, G. (1949) *The Concept of Mind*. Chicago, IL: University of Chicago Press.

Schumpeter, J.A. (1968) *The Theory of Economic Development: An Inquiry into Profits, Capital, Interest and the Capital Cycle*. Cambridge, MA: Harvard University Press.

Schön, D.A. (1983) *The Reflective Practitioner: How Professionals Think in Action*. New York: Basic Books.

Schön, D.A. (1987) *Educating the Reflective Practitioner*. San Francisco, CA: Jossey-Bass.

Simon, H.A. (1991) 'Bounded Rationality and Organizational Learning'. *Organization Science* 2: 125–34.

Slaughter, S. and Leslie, L.L. (1997) *Academic Capitalism: Politics, Policies, and the Entrepreneurial University*. Baltimore, MD: Johns Hopkins University Press.

Slaughter, S. and Rhoades, G. (2004) *Academic Capitalism and the New Economy: Markets, State, and Higher Education*, Baltimore, MD: Johns Hopkins University Press.

Sotarauta, M. (2009) 'Power and Influence Tactics in the Promotion of Regional Development: An Empirical Analysis of the Work of Finnish Regional Development Officers'. *Geoforum* 40: 895–905.

Sotarauta, M. (2010) 'Regional Development and Regional Networks: The Role of Regional Development Officers in Finland'. *European Urban and Regional Studies* 17: 387–400.

Sotarauta, M. (2012) 'Policy Learning and the "Cluster-flavoured Innovation Policy" in Finland'. *Environment and Planning C* 30: 780–95.

Sotarauta, M. and Pulkkinen, R. (2011) 'Institutional Entreprenurship for Knowledge Regions: In Search of a Fresh Set of Questions for Regional Innovation Studies'. *Environment and Planning C* 29: 96–112.

Sotarauta, M., Horlings, I. and Liddle, J. (2012) 'Leadership and Sustainable Regional Development'. In: Sotarauta, M., Horlings, I. and Liddle, J. (eds) *Leadership and Change in Sustainable Regional Development*. London: Routledge, 1–19.

Spender, J.-C. (1994) 'Knowing, Managing and Learning: A Dynamic Managerial Epistemology'. *Management Learning* 25: 387–412.

Styhre, A. (2003) *Understanding Knowledge Management: Critical and Postmodern Perspectives*. Copenhagen: Liber Abstrakt Copenhagen Business School Press.

Svensson, L. and Nielsen, K.A. (2006) 'A Framework for the Book'. In: Nielsen, K.A. and Svennson, L. (eds) *Action Research and Interactive Research Beyond Practice and Theory* Maastricht: Shaker Publishing.

Svensson, L., Ellström, P.-E. and Brulin, G. (2007) 'Introduction: On Interactive Research'. *International Journal of Action Research* 3: 233–49.

Tödtling, F. and Trippl, M. (2005) 'One Size Fits All? Towards a Differentiated Regional Innovation Policy Approach'. *Research Policy* 34: 1,203–19.

Toulmin, S. and Gustavsen, B. (1996) *Beyond Theory: Changing Organizations through Participation*. Amsterdam: John Benjamins.

Trippl, M. and Tödtling, F. (2007) 'Developing Biotechnology Clusters in Non-high Technology Regions': The Case of Austria. *Industry and Innovation* 14: 47–67.

Uyarra, E. (2010) 'What is Evolutionary About "Regional Systems of Innovation"? Implications for Regional Policy'. *Journal of Evolutionary Economics* 20: 115–37.

Weick, K.E. and Roberts, K.H. (1993) 'Collective Mind in Organizations: Heedful Interrelating on Flight Decks'. *Administrative Science Quarterly* 38: 357–81.

Wittgenstein, L. (1953) *Philosophical Investigation*. London: Blackwell.

Wollebæk, D. and Segaard, S.B. (2011) 'Sosial kapital: Hva er det og hvor kommer det fra?' In: Wollebæk, D. and Segaard, S.B. (eds) *Sosial kapital i Norge*. Oslo: Cappelen Damm Akademisk, pp. 25–49.

Index

References to figures and tables are in **bold**.

For Product Safety Concerns and Information please contact our EU
representative GPSR@taylorandfrancis.com
Taylor & Francis Verlag GmbH, Kaufingerstraße 24, 80331 München, Germany

9 7 8 1 1 3 8 2 7 1 9 8 2